KINGDOM MEN
RISING

DEVOTIONAL

KINGDOM MEN
RISING

DEVOTIONAL

DR. TONY EVANS

BETHANYHOUSE
a division of Baker Publishing Group
Minneapolis, Minnesota

© 2021 by Dr. Tony Evans

Published by Bethany House Publishers
11400 Hampshire Avenue South
Bloomington, Minnesota 55438
www.bethanyhouse.com

Bethany House Publishers is a division of
Baker Publishing Group, Grand Rapids, Michigan

Printed in China

Library of Congress Cataloging-in-Publication Data
Names: Evans, Tony, author. | Evans, Tony, Kingdom men rising.
Title: Kingdom men rising devotional / Tony Evans.
Description: Minneapolis, Minnesota : Bethany House Publishers, [2021] |
Identifiers: LCCN 2021015652 | ISBN 9780764238840
Subjects: LCSH: Christian men—Religious life. | Christian men—Prayers
    and devotions. | Spiritual formation—Prayers and devotions. | Discipling
    (Christianity)—Prayers and devotions.
Classification: LCC BV4528.2 .E9183 2021 | DDC 242/.642—dc23
LC record available at https://lccn.loc.gov/2021015652

Scripture quotations taken from the (NASB®) New American Standard Bible®,
Copyright © 1960, 1971, 1977, 1995, 2020 by The Lockman Foundation. Used by
permission. All rights reserved. www.lockman.org

Some material in chapters 9, 13, 14, and 15 adapted from Tony Evans, *America:
Turning a Nation to God* (Chicago: Moody, 2015), chapter 2.

Some material in chapters 40, 42, 43, 44, and 45 adapted from *30 Days to Overcoming Addictive Behavior*, Copyright © 2017 by Tony Evans. Published by Harvest
House Publishers, Eugene, Oregon 97408. www.harvesthousepublishers.com

Some material in chapters 41 and 42 adapted from *It's Not Too Late*, Copyright
© 2012 by Tony Evans. Published by Harvest House Publishers, Eugene, Oregon
97408. www.harvesthousepublishers.com

Some material in chapters 52, 55, and 56 adapted from Tony Evans, *Oneness Embraced* (Chicago, Moody, 2015), chapter 2.

Some material in chapter 83 adapted from Tony Evans, *Raising Kingdom Kids:
Giving Your Child a Living Faith* (Carol Stream, IL: Focus on the Family book
published by Tyndale, 2014), chapter 11.

Cover design by Dan Pitts

24 25 26 27   7 6 5 4 3 2

> Then God said, "Let Us make man in Our image, according to Our likeness; and let them rule over the fish of the sea and over the birds of the sky and over the cattle and over all the earth, and over every creeping thing that creeps on the earth."
>
> Genesis 1:26

God created the man prior to creating the woman, like pouring a foundation first, because the success or failure of God's created purpose of building His kingdom in history would be directly related to a man's relationship with and submission to God's rule over his life. Foundations don't have to be fancy or pretty, but they do have to be strong. When a foundation is weak, everything resting on it is at risk. God holds the man ultimately responsible for holding up what He has entrusted to his care while simultaneously advancing His kingdom program.

If God can get His men to pursue an intimate relationship with Him while simultaneously representing Him in all we do, He will reverse the downward spiral of the culture. God is waiting on His kingdom men to rise from our spiritual slumber and accept the responsibility of reversing the decay and disunity that engulf us.

Just as the first Adam brought defeat to the human race, the last Adam, Jesus Christ, came to bring victory. It's time for God's men, under the lordship of Jesus Christ, to change the trajectory of our culture as we submit ourselves to Him and His kingdom agenda.

ACTION

1. Assess your personal foundation on a scale of 1–10.

   _____

2. What practice can you put in place to strengthen the foundation you provide to those around you?

3. Name one thing you are willing to do this week in order to start heading in that direction.

PRAYER

Jesus, open my eyes to the truth of where I am strong and where I am weak as a man. Help me to have the humility that is necessary to shore up the foundation and fill in the cracks where it is needed most. I ask for greater wisdom and strength as I pursue You and Your role for me to rise up as a kingdom man so that I can have a positive impact on the culture and on those I love. In Your name, amen.

Bear one another's burdens, and thereby fulfill the law of Christ.

Galatians 6:2

Awakening our biblical manhood requires the commitment and the discipline to honor God in all we do. But what we often forget is that this determination is frequently formed in us over the course of our lives. It doesn't just appear out of nowhere. We are in this together. Nothing difficult we overcome ever rests solely on our own shoulders. That's one reason God emphasizes unity and the power of fellowship and discipleship throughout Scripture.

If you saw the film series *The Lord of the Rings*, you likely remember one of the most famous scenes. It comes toward the end of *The Return of the King*. The main character, Frodo, whose role it was to carry the burden of the evil ring to its destruction and thus save the world, had lost all strength. He lay unable to move forward. If he didn't make it to the top of the mountain to throw the ring in the fire, the quest would be lost.

That's when his companion, Sam, made a bold move. Scooping Frodo up in his arms and lifting him onto his back, he carried Frodo when he could no longer move forward on his own. "Come on, Mr. Frodo," he says with all the strength he can muster. "I can't carry it for you, but I can carry you."[1] Similarly, we as men may not be able to carry each other's burdens, but we can do our part to lift, encourage, support, and draw near to those in need to help them finish the task of overcoming any evil that seeks to defeat them.

ACTION

1. Identify hesitancies you have toward helping other men carry their burdens.

2. In what ways can you overcome these hesitancies in order to fulfill your role as a kingdom man?

3. What are some hindrances that keep men from accepting someone else's help, and in what ways do you identify with these?

PRAYER

Jesus, I want to be a greater help to other men in need. Show me how I can strengthen my own walk with You in order to be better positioned to help someone else. Give me wisdom on how I can use the gifts and grace You have given to me to support, encourage, and lift up men around me. In Your name, amen.

For we do not preach ourselves but Christ Jesus as Lord, and ourselves as your bond-servants for Jesus' sake.

2 Corinthians 4:5

We need kingdom men who are willing to invest not only in their own personal growth and opportunities, but also in others'. We need men who are willing to sacrifice time and effort to unleash someone else's potential. We are in this thing called life together. That's how we make it. That's how we man up. That's how we change the world for God and for good. We do it by living out the definition of a kingdom man: "a male who visibly and consistently submits to the comprehensive relationship and rule of God, underneath the Lordship of Jesus Christ, in every area of his life."[1]

A kingdom man accepts his responsibilities under God and faithfully carries them out. These responsibilities include caring for his family, serving in his church, and being present to positively impact others around him. When he is faithful to do these things, and more, God moves even pagan powers and other forces on earth to support him in advancing the kingdom agenda. God brings upon him the blessings and favor He promised to Abraham years ago.

When a kingdom man lives according to his designed purpose, he joins with other men in influencing culture, politics, entertainment, and more through intentional discipleship. This process produces kingdom disciples who then go and do the same. The process becomes cyclical, leading to multigenerational impact.

ACTION

1. Write the definition of a kingdom man where you can look at it over the course of the next week. Seek to memorize this definition.

2. What are some practical examples of consistently submitting to God's comprehensive rule over every area of life?

3. Name one area where you do not consistently submit to God's rule and identify one way you can seek to change that.

Jesus, I desire and intend to live as a kingdom man who consistently submits to the comprehensive relationship and rule of God underneath Your lordship in every area of my life. I do not always live up to this desire, so I ask for Your mercy and grace for those times I do not. Show me also how to extend mercy and grace to myself so that I do not live in guilt and shame for falling short. In Your name, amen.

FOUR

Brethren, join in following my example, and observe those who walk according to the pattern you have in us.

Philippians 3:17

As kingdom men, we must grab hold of those who need to be shown a better way, rather than write them off. Paul told Timothy and others in his sphere of influence that they were to follow his example as he followed Christ (see 1 Corinthians 11:1 and Philippians 3:17). Keep in mind that to have an example to follow means you must have someone setting one. This requires living in a spiritually mature manner and guiding others in how to do likewise. It takes both: ongoing personal discipline and intentional investment in others.

While many of us are waiting on God to fix what is wrong, He is waiting on us to step up as men of faith and do what is right. He is waiting on men who don't just talk about faith but also walk in it. These are the men whose actions demonstrate that they truly believe in the God they claim to worship.

One way we do this is through intentional investments in relationships as well as mutual learning in a spiritual context. The more formal term for this is *discipleship*. We are to live as kingdom disciples pursuing the making of more kingdom disciples throughout our communities, our nation, and the world.

A kingdom disciple can be defined as a believer who takes part in the spiritual development of progressively learning to live all of life under the lordship of Jesus Christ and then seeks to replicate that process in others. As this is done, God's kingdom agenda marches forward on earth.

ACTION

1. Write out the definition of a kingdom disciple where you can look at it over the course of the next week. Seek to memorize this definition.

2. In what ways can you seek to "replicate the process" of discipleship in others?

3. Why is it important to disciple others?

PRAYER

Jesus, motivate my heart to follow you more closely and to replicate Your will and ways in those around me. Inspire me to be more intentional about impacting others for good and Your glory. Encourage me through allowing me to see the fruit of this impact when and where I can. In Your name, amen.

FIVE

> Roam to and fro through the streets of Jerusalem, and look now and take note. And seek in her open squares, if you can find a man, if there is one who does justice, who seeks truth, then I will pardon her.
>
> Jeremiah 5:1

Over and over God has called men to intervene on behalf of a dying land. Ezekiel 22:30 records it this way, "I searched for a man among them who would build up the wall and stand in the gap before Me for the land, so that I would not destroy it; but I found no one." The land had plenty of males, but God couldn't find a man. There's a big difference between being a male and being a kingdom man. You can be one without the other when you refuse to take responsibility under God.

Taking responsibility means owning the issues that show up in your life and in the lives of your loved ones. It starts by removing the word *blame* from your vocabulary. No matter who is at fault, it is your role to fix it. That's what a kingdom man does. To blame someone else only leads to bitterness. Bitterness then gives birth to other sins like anger, resentment, and even betrayal.

God is searching for men who will stand in the gap for their families, churches, communities, and land. Standing in the gap requires courage. It requires personal responsibility. It requires a removal of blame, finger-pointing, and a victim mentality. Once we put these mind-sets aside, we are better positioned to create favorable outcomes for ourselves and those we love and shepherd.

ACTION

1. If God were to search our nation for men who would stand in the gap so He would not destroy us, how many do you think He would find?

2. Would you be someone God would consider as one who "does justice" and who "seeks truth"?

3. What does it look like in everyday life to "do justice" or to "seek truth"?

PRAYER

Jesus, help me gain a better understanding of what it means to do justice and seek truth according to Your Word. I want to be a kingdom man who stands in the gap and who You call on when intervention is needed in our land. Open my heart and train my ears to hear You more clearly so I can live for you and Your kingdom agenda. In Your name, amen.

SIX

> He has told you, O man, what is good; and what does the
> LORD require of you but to do justice, to love kindness,
> and to walk humbly with your God?
>
> Micah 6:8

God regularly instructed His men on the crucial importance of two aspects of life: righteousness and justice (Exodus 34). *Righteousness* is the moral standard that should govern every man's life and choices. *Justice* is the equitable application of God's moral standard as demonstrated in society.

Many people identify with and commend the need for righteousness. But not as many understand why justice is similarly as vital. This has caused a condensed approach to discipleship and cultural influence by believers today, resulting in little overall societal impact.

Kingdom men, it is our role to seek out the manifestation of justice in our culture. We are to rise up for those who cannot do so on their own (Micah 6:8; Proverbs 31:8). We do this by ensuring fair treatment and equal opportunities for the meeting of basic human needs such as education and employment. Without opportunity, many people lose hope. And one of the primary problems we are facing today is an increased sense of hopelessness.

That's why we need men who will be committed not only to evangelizing people for heaven but also to improving people's lives on earth. The kingdom of God involves both heaven and earth. We impact the culture at large when we influence individuals nearby.

ACTION

1. Describe in your own terms the difference between righteousness and justice.

2. Which one do you see yourself pursuing more regularly, for yourself and others?

3. What is one thing you can do to increase your ability to live out both aspects simultaneously?

PRAYER

Jesus, You have instructed us to pursue a life that honors the principles of both righteousness and justice. It's not one without the other. Neither does one eclipse the other. Help me to understand how I need to grow as a kingdom disciple in order to be able to fully represent the King and His kingdom in both areas well. In Your name, amen.

SEVEN

For it is God who is at work in you, both to will and to work for His good pleasure.

Philippians 2:13

You have been created by God with a specific post He wants you to fulfill and a purpose He wants you to live out. He has scouted you, pursued you, and drafted you for His kingdom team. You have a divinely orchestrated reason for your manhood. Now, I know the culture wants to give you a whole slew of other reasons for being a man, but God says clearly that He created you for something great.

Granted, that purpose may seem elusive right now. You may have to search for it like the Avengers searched for the Infinity Stones. But if you will search for it, you will find it. Instead of looking for your purpose, look for God. After all, He knows your purpose. Once you find Him and become intimate with Him, He will reveal it to you.

God has placed your purpose in you, in seed form. You grow that seed through an intentional pursuit of Him. When you learn His ways like an athlete learns the plays, desires, and instincts of a coach, you will align yourself with all that is needed to maximize your potential. Your effort involves aligning yourself within His grid and with His design. God will bring about your greatness. You don't need to force it, manipulate to get it, or obsessively work toward it. Draw close to God, and God will fulfill your purpose both for you and through you.

ACTION

1. Describe your approach to "pursuing" an intimate relationship with God.

2. In what ways can you strengthen this approach?

3. What one thing from your answer to the previous question are you willing to implement this week?

PRAYER

Jesus, help me not to get distracted by pursuing my purpose rather than looking to You, because You know why I am here and what I am to accomplish. You know what I need to do to experience the greatest fulfillment of my personal destiny. Draw me near to You and enable me to know You more fully and hear You more clearly every day. In Your name, amen.

DAY

EIGHT

A plan in the heart of a man is like deep water, but a man of understanding draws it out.

Proverbs 20:5

An authentic spiritual life doesn't come through rituals, budgets, programs, buildings, or even religion. Spiritual life, power, and strength come from the Spirit. The closer you are to the Spirit, the more abundant life you experience and the more influence you have (John 10:10; 15:7). The further you drift from Christ's Spirit, the more death and decay you experience in the various aspects of your life.

An important part of maturing spiritually comes from healing in those areas that hold you back. Forgiveness frees you from the slavery of self-pity and blame. Both make you ineffective for the kingdom of God. You must intentionally pursue personal spiritual growth, maturity, and mental and spiritual health if you are to have a lasting impact on the lives you touch.

As we all grow and develop individually, it will enable us to identify, own, and address the issues plaguing us on many fronts today, culturally and as the body of Christ. As kingdom men, we must own our roles in guiding others to the one true King. We must own the responsibility of calling a culture in decline back to Christ. It's time we awaken not only ourselves but also the culture at large, so that we will take to the field and overcome the enemy's opposition.

ACTION

1. On a scale of 1–10, how much of the spiritual "abundant life" do you feel you are experiencing?

2. What things can you do in order to move that number higher on the scale?

3. Why is spiritual maturity an ongoing pursuit rather than a one-time goal?

PRAYER

Jesus, draw out the plans You have for me from the depths of my understanding into the forefront of my awareness. Help me to see the swiftest route to spiritual maturity so that I can take it fully without fail. Give me grace to grow and experience all that I am meant to be, for Your glory and others' good. In Your name, amen.

NINE

> The hand of the LORD was upon me, and He brought me out by the Spirit of the LORD and set me down in the middle of the valley; and it was full of bones. He caused me to pass among them round about, and behold, there were very many on the surface of the valley; and lo, they were very dry. He said to me, "Son of man, can these bones live?" And I answered, "O Lord GOD, You know."
>
> Ezekiel 37:1–3

A valley is a low place. It's that place where you have to look up just to see the bottom. The biblical account of Ezekiel and an army of skeletons can be compared to a valley. The bones in Ezekiel's valley jumbled together like too many things stuffed in a drawer, nothing connected as it should be.

I don't expect you to identify literally with Ezekiel's account, or with dismembered bones. But if you think about the meaning behind the story, you may be able to identify with it. Because many men live dismembered lives. They don't see hope. Their lives—hopes, dreams, relationships—feel broken. There seems to be no light at the end of the tunnel unless it's the light of an oncoming train.

When questions come up about how to cure the plague of missing biblical manhood in our nation that leads to so many societal ills, most responses come with a shrug of the shoulders. Far too many Christian men are broken. Ezekiel's own words when he was asked if the skeletons could ever rise up may reflect our own. To paraphrase, "Only God knows" (v. 3). That's a polite way of saying, "I don't think any of us knows how to solve this. At all." But if you read further, Ezekiel's story does bring hope. But only when he learns to look to God, and God alone, for the solution to life's struggles.

ACTION

1. Can you identify an area or areas in your life that feel like these dry bones?
2. What would it take for you to hope again that God can restore, revive, and redeem what has been broken or lost?
3. Take a moment to ask God to do that.

PRAYER

Jesus, show me the life that can be given to the areas of my life that seem dead, dismembered, broken, or lost. Remind me of Your power. Restore my shaken faith. Let me know that it is okay to hope again and believe again because You are able to do exceedingly beyond what I could ask or even imagine. In Your name, amen.

> Then He said to me, "Son of man, these bones are the whole house of Israel; behold, they say, 'Our bones are dried up and our hope has perished. We are completely cut off.'"
>
> Ezekiel 37:11

Many men lack answers for how to address the issues in their lives. What's more, they lack the assurance of faith that what seems broken in their lives, homes, and nation could ever be restored. Perhaps it's a broken marriage. Could be a dead-end career. Might be a miserable mentality. We are certainly witnessing a disastrous moral framework not only in our society but in our entertainment, in our music, and often in our churches and our own lives as well. Yet whatever has caused so many men's Christian strength to lie limp on the ground seems to have sucked away hope for a solution as well. Maybe that describes you.

If that's you, I would argue that hope has gone primarily because it's hard to fix a problem when you don't know, or choose to ignore, the cause. Hope leaves when we focus on the symptoms and not on the sins that brought the symptoms about. Whenever you are looking for a cure, you must address the cause. Far too many laymen, pastors, and politicians are doing patchwork on symptoms rather than dealing with the systemic roots that have caused the decay. If we are ever to get our lives, homes, churches, and nation right, we have to address the spiritual causes beneath the brokenness. We'll look at some possible causes in the upcoming devotions.

ACTION

1. What happens when you fail to address the cause of a sickness?

2. Describe how that also applies to spiritual sicknesses such as sin.

3. Is there an area in your life where you haven't identified the cause of the troubles you face, which has kept you from either healing or overcoming?

PRAYER

Jesus, I want to address the cause of any trials or chaos in my life, family, church, and community. I don't want to keep trying to make the symptoms go away without looking at how to fix the problem once and for all. Give me the courage to peel back the layers of deception or denial that have prevented me from rooting out the cause of sin and its effect in many areas. In Your name, amen.

ELEVEN

> But your iniquities have made a separation between you
> and your God, and your sins have hidden His face from
> you so that He does not hear.
>
> Isaiah 59:2

One reason you can feel like your life is dried up in a valley for an extended time is because of disobedience to God. Disobedience creates spiritual distance. And any distance from God will lead to a disastrous level of spiritual dryness. It can be subtle at first. You may start off on whatever it is you are doing with good intentions, but if you turn from God along the way, you begin to rebel. Because it is subtle, it may not feel like rebellion. It may just feel like you are drifting away from God and His plan and purpose. But the result remains: You become spiritually estranged. In doing so, you remove or reduce your fellowship with God and devolve into a life composed of piles of dry bones.

If that sounds like you in any way, if you are dry—spiritually, emotionally, relationally, or in any other way—it is most likely because you are distant from God. And disobedience always leads to distance. Now, I know that we all have dry times. A man can face a slump here or setback there. I'm not talking about that. But if you find yourself living in a dry valley where every single day you wake up to no motivation, no passion, and no spiritual fervor, it is because you have become distant from God. One thing leads to prolonged distance from God: failing to align yourself under the rule of the King.

ACTION

1. Examine your spiritual closeness to God and rate it on a scale of 1–10, with 10 being very close. _____
2. How do you think relational distance from God has affected your life?
3. In what ways do you think drawing closer to God could bring improvements into your life?

PRAYER

Jesus, forgive me for having pulled back from Your will and Your way over the course of my life. Forgive me for every left turn I have taken. Reveal to me what I need to do to draw nearer to You and light the spark of intimacy between us. In Your name, amen.

TWELVE

Then they will cry out to the LORD, but He will not answer them. Instead, He will hide His face from them at that time because they have practiced evil deeds.

Micah 3:4

One way to become distant from God is through idolatry. Now, I know that most of you reading this think that you don't worship idols. You are probably imagining worshiping a statue, nature, or something else set up as a false god. But idolatry isn't just bowing down to a carved statue stuck on a pole. No, an idol is anything that usurps God's rightful rule in your life. Idols come in all shapes and sizes. An idol could be sports, technology, entertainment, or any number of things. Idols can even be found in the church.

Idolatry is not just an out-there concept in a distant land. I say that because idolatry centers on alignment: That which you align your thoughts, words, and actions under is what you value most.

Have you ever wondered how we can have all these churches and all these books and all these songs, programs, seminars, huddle groups, Bible studies, radio broadcasts, podcasts, and more and yet still have all this mess? There are idols everywhere; that's how. Somebody, or something, has been brought into God's realm of rule, and there is no room for two kings in any sovereign land. Anytime you turn to other sources to meet your needs or to solve your problems with alternate solutions, you have become an idolater. As a result, your life has been set on a path to symbolically lay dormant in a wasteland of a dismembered destiny.

ACTION

1. What or who are some things, people, or activities in your life that usurp God's rightful rule and influence over you?

2. Have you seen any negative fallout by placing these above God's rule?

3. In what areas would you like to see God have greater influence over your life?

PRAYER

Jesus, reveal to me those areas where I have sinned and placed something else, or even someone else, above Your rule in my life. Show me the negative results so I can be fully aware of what I have brought upon myself and can learn from it. Help me to draw closer to You and let go of any idols. In Your name, amen.

DAY

THIRTEEN

> "Therefore prophesy and say to them, 'Thus says the Lord God, "Behold, I will open your graves and cause you to come up out of your graves, My people; and I will bring you into the land of Israel. Then you will know that I am the Lord, when I have opened your graves and caused you to come up out of your graves, My people."'"
>
> Ezekiel 37:12–13

When you have drifted away from God—like the Israelites in Ezekiel 37—you can find yourself in a situation with no solution. Any spiritual disconnect can lead to a social, familial, or individual catastrophe. This happens when you are so far removed from God that you can no longer readily identify the cause of the effect. When you fail to make the connection between the spiritual and the social, you will also fail to seek the solution that can bring real and lasting impact.

A failure to address the spiritual root of the physical mayhem will result in remaining in a valley of spiritual, emotional, relational, or even vocational dryness, unable to rise at all.

Yet in the midst of any problem, we can find a promise. In the Israelites' situation, God made a promise that

He alone would open the graves and cause life to exist where death had once dominated. Last I checked, if you are dead and you come up out of a grave, that's a supernatural rising. Thus, the good news of this promise is that no matter how dry you are or how dry your situation is, those bones can live again. If you are dry spiritually, you can live again. If your marriage has been dried up for years or decades, it can thrive again. If your circumstances are dry or your career is a wasteland, it can rise and prosper again.

If God can take an ossuary of dry bones and cause it to pulsate with life, how much more can He do for you? The question is never *Can God do it?* The question is always *How badly do you want it?*

ACTION

1. Do you believe God can reverse irreversible situations and produce life where there was only death?
2. Is there an area in your life where you would like to see this happen?
3. Take some time to ask God to intervene and turn things around for you.

Jesus, I believe You have the power to raise up that which appears to be over and done with. Reveal this power in my own life and show me what I need to do to cooperate with You in this process of restoration. In Your name, amen.

FOURTEEN

So Jesus was saying to those Jews who had believed Him, "If you continue in My word, then you are truly disciples of Mine; and you will know the truth, and the truth will make you free."

John 8:31–32

You've probably had your car battery go out at some point. I know I have. Standing there looking at that battery won't do a bit of good. Talking to the battery won't change a thing either. It's only when you take a set of cables to connect your dead battery to someone else's live battery that you get the spark you need to drive. That battery gets recharged through the transference of life from another.

Similarly, the only way that we as kingdom men will experience personal awakening and rise up to fulfill our destinies is through connecting to God's living Word and Spirit. Both are essential before we can experience the spiritual resurrection God offers. It's through His life transferred to us that we will have a transformative influence on our homes, communities, nation, and even world.

It's truth that sets a man free. Not our version of truth—but the truth itself. We discover the truth through reading, learning, and applying God's Word. Sometimes God has to allow us to reach a point of personal paralysis or collective chaos before we will be willing to listen to truth at all.

ACTION

1. How satisfied are you with the level of engagement you have in God's Word?
2. What is one simple strategy you can apply this week to increase your engagement?
3. Describe the difference between the truth of God and culture's so-called "my truth."

PRAYER

Jesus, make me know You and the truth of the living Word like I never have before. Show me all that I can do to grow in my understanding of truth and in the wisdom of applying it to my life. Show me how to better serve You in everything I do. In Your name, amen.

But Jesus answered and said to them, "You are mistaken, not understanding the Scriptures nor the power of God."

Matthew 22:29

It is God's Word that is to order our lives when we read and apply it. Keep in mind that reading it isn't enough. Memorizing it isn't enough. We must apply the truth of God's Word to our decisions in order to receive the benefit obedience brings.

When you choose to live in alignment with the truth and God's precepts, and when you serve in your home, your church, and your community, the nation feels the effect. It is when kingdom men—as individuals, business owners, employees, politicians, fathers, medical workers, preachers, and the like—all align with God and His Word that we experience order in the land.

But remember, only the Spirit of God himself can pull anything up out of its deadened or hopeless situation. That means your top priority right now ought to be cultivating and growing in your relationship with God's Word and getting to know Him better. As you do, you'll awaken. You'll stand. Nothing, and no one, is too far gone from God's powerful hand. He wants you to know that. In fact, that's why God does the supernatural. He revives and restores so that you will recognize His powerful hand and come to know Him more.

ACTION

1. Why is it important to consistently remain in a state of learning when it comes to God's Word?

2. Are you satisfied with how much you pursue the knowing and applying of God's Word?

3. What would help you be more motivated to seek God's Word and apply it?

PRAYER

Jesus, help me to not get so caught up in pursuing busy things that I forget to go to Your Word for wisdom, direction, and understanding. As I read Your Word, I also ask that You will enlighten my heart and my mind with insight. Show me what I need to apply, especially in those areas where I have gotten off track. In Your name, amen.

"Behold, I am laying in Zion a stone, a tested stone, a costly cornerstone for the foundation, firmly placed. He who believes in it will not be disturbed."

Isaiah 28:16

Everyone knows how important the foundation of a home is. If you wind up with cracks in your walls, it is usually due to a faulty or shifting foundation. Today there are metaphorical cracks all around us. Cracks in our families. Cracks with our kids. There are cracks in our direction, economics, relationships, politics, and careers. There are also racial cracks. Class cracks. And, of course, religious cracks. Cracks have broken out everywhere around and among us. As a result, we spend a great amount of our time, money, and energy trying to patch up the cracks to make things look better. For a while they do look better. But before long we discover that, given enough time, the cracks reappear.

This is because the foundation keeps moving. The foundation has not been solidified. Any structure that stands on a weak foundation will have cracks in its walls. Any life standing on the same will become rife with its own brokenness as well.

This isn't new information. Take sports, for example. Every athlete knows that to be successful you have to strengthen the core. The core, your foundation, controls your ability for movement. A stronger core allows for greater balance, reach, and overall performance. Similarly, a stronger spiritual foundation enables a successful life. Foundations aren't fancy, and foundations aren't pretty, but they had better be solid.

ACTION

1. What are some effects that a faulty spiritual foundation can produce in a person's life?
2. Are any of these effects showing up in your life?
3. What happens when a faulty foundation is left to crumble over time?

PRAYER

Jesus, it isn't ever easy to repair a foundation that is falling apart, but if it's not done, even more damage will occur. I look to You to find out how to repair the foundation of my life where it is faulty. In Your name, amen.

SEVENTEEN

"Therefore everyone who hears these words of Mine and acts on them, may be compared to a wise man who built his house on the rock. And the rain fell, and the floods came, and the winds blew and slammed against that house; and yet it did not fall, for it had been founded on the rock."

Matthew 7:24–25

In the parable in Matthew 7:24–29, we read about two very different houses. One house stood against the storm. The other house fell due to the storm. Not only did the other house fall, but Jesus emphasized that "great was its fall." It didn't just topple over. No, this house came crashing down, most likely destroying everything and everyone in its proximity.

Same storm. Different results. But why? A look at the lives and choices of these two men gives us insight. After all, common sense will tell you that you can't build a skyscraper on the foundation of a chicken coop. The higher you plan to build, the deeper and wider your foundation must be. Our problem today is that we have too many men aiming high without the necessary spiritual foundation to maintain their dreams. One wrong move, and the whole thing tumbles down like a badly balanced Jenga game.

Never forget, you are the foundation. You are the foundation for so much that happens around you. It's all banking on you and your choices. God clearly declares that men have the primary responsibility of establishing the foundation for all else around them, such as their homes, careers, relationships, vision, and even the culture at large.

ACTION

1. Describe the difference between an emotional reaction to life's storms and the faith to face the storms.

2. What ways can emotionally reacting to difficulties put you in a worse position to overcome what you are facing?

3. What do you think is the main response our culture instructs men to give to issues—an emotional reaction or a heartfelt faith?

PRAYER

Jesus, enable me not to react emotionally to difficulties I face. Help me to make it through the storms of life because I stand on the sure foundation of faith in You and Your Word. I trust in You and want that trust to rise up in me as courage. In Your name, amen.

EIGHTEEN

"Everyone who hears these words of Mine and does not act on them, will be like a foolish man who built his house on the sand. The rain fell, and the floods came, and the winds blew and slammed against that house; and it fell— and great was its fall."

Matthew 7:26–27

As you read the parable of the two men and their houses, it's important to note that in Scripture, a house can symbolically refer to one of four different things:

1. **Individual:** Kingdom men pursue personal purpose and aim to leave a lasting impact.
2. **Family:** Kingdom men seek to impact their homes in such a way that all within them grow to be mature, responsible believers in Christ.
3. **Church:** Kingdom men concern themselves with the spiritual footprint they are making with their lives.
4. **Society:** Kingdom men involve themselves in the structural entities that govern a land so as to influence the culture for Christ.

Both of these men dreamed of building a house. Therefore, both men housed in their hearts a desire for personal development, familial influence, ministry impact, and societal good. They wanted a life of significance. A family that was strong. A ministry that was effective. And a culture that was ordered well. Kingdom men desire nothing less. Yet these men went about their desires differently, and this showed up in the results. One man's house stood. The other man's house fell hard.

ACTION

1. Out of the four areas outlined above, which is your strongest and which is your weakest area of including God's wisdom in your pursuits?
2. Why do you think you are weakest in the area you listed as that?
3. What is one thing you can do to strengthen your application of God's wisdom in the area you listed as your weakest?

PRAYER

Jesus, I want to serve You in all areas of my life—not just in the ones that come easy to me. This includes my personal life, my family relationships, the church I attend, and the society I live in. Open my eyes to see how I can better integrate Your wisdom into each of these areas. In Your name, amen.

NINETEEN

"These things I have spoken to you, so that in Me you may have peace. In the world you have tribulation, but take courage; I have overcome the world."

John 16:33

Did you know that a storm in Scripture often does not refer to a literal storm? It often refers to an adverse set of circumstances. When the Bible speaks of a storm, the writer may be conveying negative events entering into a life. A storm connotes trouble, tribulation, and trials. Storms seek to knock you over—mentally, emotionally, physically, and spiritually. You are either in a storm, just heading out of a storm, or about to experience a storm. This is because life is full of troubles, as our passage for today reminds us. That's just the way it is. Storms tear through towns as well as lives, and frequently at that. It's going to rain, thunder, and hail. On everyone. Both the righteous and the unrighteous are affected by storms.

Storms don't care how much you earn or even what you do. Hail is hail, and it will dent any car it hits. Wind is wind, and it will destroy any building its tornadic forces push against. Rain is rain, and when it floods it doesn't ask your permission or level of prominence first.

Storms affect us all. Just as they affected the two men's shared vision of a brighter tomorrow in the parable found in Matthew 7:24–29. That's why it is more important to focus on your response to life's storms than to seek to remove them. A kingdom man must build his life, home, family, and more on the solid foundation of God's Word if he is to withstand the storms that blow through life itself.

ACTION

1. Do you feel that you are well prepared for life's storms?

2. When things get difficult, do you find you react more and lose sight of any game plan you had previously set in place?

3. How can you shift from emotional reactions to spiritual responses in life's difficulties?

PRAYER

Jesus, rather than living in denial that storms happen, I want to be spiritually prepared for when they do. Help me devise a solid game plan to approach life's troubles and tribulations from a position of strength. In Your name, amen.

But prove yourselves doers of the word, and not merely hearers who delude themselves.

James 1:22

The parable of the two men in Matthew 7:24–29 reflects a lot of us today. Many men are asking questions such as, What does it mean to build a life on a solid foundation? How do I create something lasting? Should I build high or wide? Should I go this direction or that? This career or that one? Work this many hours, or that many? Questions like these pummel men's minds like pellets of hail in a hot summer storm. The rat race has us all running on a wheel at times. But Jesus gives us the answer to all of this and more when He tells us how we can each choose to live as the wise man or the fool. It's simple:

"Therefore everyone who hears these words of Mine and acts on them, may be compared to a wise man."

verse 24

"Everyone who hears these words of Mine and does not act on them, will be like a foolish man."

verse 26

For starters, Jesus is assuming one thing. He's assuming you're hearing His words. But hearing is never solely the answer. A running back might hear the play called that requires him to rush behind the quarterback to grab the ball. He might hear it clearly. But if he doesn't do it—if he fails to execute the play—the play is most likely over. It's never in the hearing alone. It's always in the doing that makes a man great. The difference between a strong foundation and a weak one is not merely information. You can have a PhD in information but still be a fool. The difference lies in whether you know how and are willing to apply the information you heard. That's wisdom.

ACTION

1. Describe the difference between a hearer of the word and a doer of the word.

2. What are some things Satan uses to try to keep men from living as doers of the Word?

3. How can you overcome Satan's strategies to keep you ineffective for God's kingdom?

Jesus, I want to be a doer of Your Word. I want to live with wisdom in my choices. This starts with a greater level of discernment. Please give me wisdom and discernment so I will know the right choices to make. Then, give me the courage to make them. In Your name, amen.

TWENTY-ONE

> Therefore, take up the full armor of God, so that you will be able to resist in the evil day, and having done every-thing, to stand firm. Stand firm therefore, having girded your loins with truth, and having put on the breastplate of righteousness, and having shod your feet with the preparation of the gospel of peace; in addition to all, taking up the shield of faith with which you will be able to extinguish all the flaming arrows of the evil one. And take the helmet of salvation, and the sword of the Spirit, which is the word of God.
>
> Ephesians 6:13–17

When God did spectacular things in the Bible, He al-ways required the people He was working through to do something first. He told Moses to hold out his rod. He told Joshua to have the priests step into the water. Jesus told those at the tomb of Lazarus to move the stone. He told the disciples to bring what they could find to eat to feed five thousand. Over and over again God would tell a person, or a group of people, to do something that would then activate the power of His Word.

The reason a lot of men are not seeing God move miraculously in their lives is that God is not seeing them move in an act of faith. By the way, attending church does not count as an act of faith. Simply hearing the Word will never produce the supernatural intervention of God in your circumstances. Until He detects obedience to and alignment with what He said, you're pretty much on your own. God's authority to overcome obstacles or move you forward in your dreams is activated by action, not talk.

Living as a kingdom man requires you to live by actions that demonstrate your faith in God. The days of passive Christianity are long gone. It is time to stand up for what you believe in, and you do that through your choices.

ACTION

1. Identify something God has asked you to do in the past in faith but that you did not do.
2. What was the result of your lack of action?
3. Why do you think God wants to see you demonstrate faith through an action before He will show up on your behalf?

PRAYER

Jesus, help me to stay connected to Your power and strength through the armor of God. In this way, I will have all I need to be a kingdom man of actions that demonstrate my faith. I ask for God's miraculous intervention in my life and especially in the difficulties I face. In Your name, amen.

TWENTY-TWO

> "And by this you invalidated the word of God for the sake of your tradition. You hypocrites, rightly did Isaiah prophesy of you: 'This people honors Me with their lips, but their heart is far away from Me. But in vain do they worship Me, teaching as doctrines the precepts of men.'"
>
> Matthew 15:6–9

Wisdom is both the ability and the responsibility of applying God's truth to life's choices. You can only identify a wise man or a fool by his decisions. Not by the songs he sings in church. Not by the Scriptures he quotes either. Many men can speak fluent Christianese. But all that means absolutely nothing unless you are seeking outcomes through aligning spiritual truths with life's scenarios.

Biblical wisdom is about as practical a thing as you can get. It's always tied to the day-in and day-out decisions based on what a person thinks, says, and does. When you choose God by your actions, you activate the divine programming from the Word to go to work for you in bringing about good results.

Do you know what happens if you mix rock with sand? You get sandy rock. It's not solid. When you do this spiritually, it's what we know as "human wisdom." It's man's point of view with a little Jesus sprinkled on top. But any time you apply human wisdom to life's issues, you get the same disastrous result as you would if you added a bit of arsenic to your stew. When you do this, Matthew 15:6 says you have literally canceled out the power of God's Word. When you attach man's point of view to God, and when it contradicts God's point of view, you cancel out God's. Thus, you also cancel out His strength and divine intervention in your life.

ACTION

1. What are some ways our Christian culture has added "human wisdom" to God's truth?

2. What are some of the results of this mix?

3. Describe Matthew 15:6 in your own contemporary understanding.

PRAYER

Jesus, it's easy to get caught up in mixing human thoughts into Your Word and then calling it "my truth." The problem is "my truth" isn't going to be there for me when I need it to. I need You to set me free from life's troubles with the truth that has all power. I ask for this in my life. In Your name, amen.

TWENTY-THREE

For that man ought not to expect that he will receive
anything from the Lord, being a double-minded man,
unstable in all his ways.

James 1:7–8

In order to awaken to your full potential, you have to start
with a solid foundation based on the Word of God. That
means more than just knowing, studying, or memorizing
His Word. You have to act on it. The power of His promises
remains dormant unless activated by your faith through
what you do. Your foundation determines your future.

Your foundation is the Word of God *applied*. It's not
just the Word of God *known*. You will not see the intervention of God until He sees your obedience to His truth.
God is waiting on you to take your rightful place in this
world. He is waiting for you to rise to the occasion and
secure your spot of significance in His kingdom made
manifest on earth. But that only happens when you step
out—fully, faithfully, and single-mindedly—according to
the direction of His will.

I'm not suggesting that following God will keep you
from the storm. Sometimes if you follow Him, like the
disciples who sailed straight into the monstrous storm on

the Sea of Galilee, He will direct you into the eye of the storm. But what I am saying is that when you choose to live life by His truth, you will engage the programming of His Word and witness His work in the midst of the storm. The wise man in the Matthew 7:24–29 parable faced the storm. He didn't avoid the hurricane that came his way. He just withstood it. He didn't succumb to it, because he had built his life on the right foundation. You are to do the same as a kingdom man.

ACTION

1. What does being a "double-minded" man mean to you personally?

2. Have you ever known someone who was double-minded, and if so, what were some of the consequences in their life?

3. In what ways does the culture seek to make men double-minded?

PRAYER

Jesus, I do not want to live as a double-minded man. I want to live as a kingdom man making my decisions and carrying out my actions based on the truth of Your Word. Show me the way I should go in order to withstand all of life's storms. In Your name, amen.

TWENTY-FOUR

> Do not be deceived, God is not mocked; for whatever a man sows, this he will also reap. For the one who sows to his own flesh will from the flesh reap corruption, but the one who sows to the Spirit will from the Spirit reap eternal life.
>
> Galatians 6:7–8

Many men do not envision success as it really is. They envision it all culminating in fireworks, glitz, and one big resounding stadium of applause. Our entertainment industry and social media sites, along with professional sports, have created this unrealistic view of what it means to be a successful man. Unfortunately, this expectation often causes men to miss out on true success when it comes along. Or it causes them to miss out on enjoying the success they have achieved. As a result of not recognizing it, they wind up chasing the next big thing. And then the next. And the next, always spinning their wheels in the rat race of this temporal life.

A lot of the milestones of success in our lives may actually be bittersweet, when all is said and done. That's because we live in a broken world tainted by sin and its effects. But unless we realize what true success looks like and recognize what spiritual success is, we may wind up on a never-ending quest for something we've already obtained. Without a clear understanding of kingdom success, we won't know what to invest in with our time, talents, and treasures. Whatever a man sows will be what he reaps. But Satan often gets men to sow into the wrong things because of this misunderstanding of authentic success.

ACTION

1. Identify the top three things or visions you have sown into over the last few years and examine any results.
2. Do these results live up to your hopes and expectations? Why or why not?
3. In what ways can you better sow into eternal and authentic visions of kingdom success?

PRAYER

Jesus, help me to be mindful of my time and what I choose to invest in. Help me to have an authentic understanding of kingdom success so I do not end up chasing after the wind. Show me what is a waste of my time and what is a valuable thing to focus on or enjoy. In Your name, amen.

TWENTY-FIVE

> "This book of the law shall not depart from your mouth, but you shall meditate on it day and night, so that you may be careful to do according to all that is written in it; for then you will make your way prosperous, and then you will have success."
>
> Joshua 1:8

Spiritually, success is fulfilling God's purpose for your life. The biblical definition of success is living out your God-given purpose. In our culture, there are a number of errant descriptions of what it means to be successful. Some people assume that success is tied to how much money a person has. Others base it on how high up the career ladder you go. More and more these days, success is defined by how many followers you have on social media or how many likes you get. But the problem with all these assumptions is that they are not based on God's standard of success.

Jesus gave us the definition of success when He said, "I glorified You on the earth, having accomplished the work which You have given Me to do" (John 17:4).

Paul said the same thing in a different way when he penned these words: "I have fought the good fight, I have finished the course, I have kept the faith" (2 Timothy 4:7).

In fact, God told Joshua that his success was entirely based on his careful meditation on the Word of God combined with aligning his decisions and actions underneath it (see Joshua 1:8). Success involves fulfilling what God has called you to do.

ACTION

1. What is your personal description of success?
2. What would your life look like, practically and tangibly, for you to consider yourself successful?
3. What do you think is God's definition of success?

PRAYER

Jesus, help me to glorify You on earth like You glorified the Father during Your time here. Redefine for me what it means to be successful if my definition differs from Yours at all. Help me to discover the secret of being satisfied in the successes I have accomplished already. In Your name, amen.

TWENTY-SIX

> The secret of the LORD is for those who fear Him, and He
> will make them know His covenant.
>
> Psalm 25:14

Everyone wants to be a success. Nobody sets out to fail. And while none of us can go back and undo the mistakes of yesteryears, each of us has the option of becoming successful from here on out. We can either begin the journey or continue the journey of fulfilling God's destiny for us as kingdom men.

God gives us the secret to living a life of success in Psalm 25:14. To know God's covenant is to know His favor and His blessings, as God's covenant is expressly tied to His covering. Align yourself under God's relational, covenantal rule in life, and you will experience spiritual success.

But there is a condition to success that this secret reveals to us if you look at it closely enough. This condition is that you only get to know God's covenant by fearing Him. There exists a cause-and-effect scenario for achieving spiritual success. The amount of honor and respect you have for God and His Word will directly impact your level of spiritual success. You can't dishonor God in your decisions and expect to achieve any level of kingdom success. God has a standard, and He does not adjust that standard to the wiles of mankind or cultural norms.

ACTION

1. What does the term *covenant* mean to you?
2. Describe how you feel about living your life in alignment with God's covenant.
3. Is there an area of your life you need to adjust to show God a greater level of respect?

PRAYER

Jesus, show me where I am dishonoring You with decisions that are made outside of Your covenant so that I can adjust and get in alignment with You. Help me to move forward in spiritual success through the choices I make. In Your name, amen.

TWENTY-SEVEN

> The fear of the LORD is the beginning of wisdom, and the knowledge of the Holy One is understanding.
>
> Proverbs 9:10

A covenant is a spiritually binding relationship ordained by God through which He advances His kingdom. It's the mechanism through which He accomplishes His purposes, goals, and agenda. It's an arrangement of a relationship, not merely an official contract. When you are aligned with God in His covenant, you are privy to His secrets. He lets you in on things others do not know.

If you're married, you know what it's like to have secrets that you share only with your spouse. Other people have general things to discuss with you, but as a couple, you often share your innermost hopes and thoughts with each other. These are the hidden things accessible by the nature of the covenantal relationship of marriage. In fact, secrets are often so valued and guarded that they are spoken in whispers. You need to be close, not only relationally but often physically, in order to share secrets.

Accessing God's covenant through fearing Him lets you in on His secrets. It brings you close enough to

God to hear His whisper. God unveils His purposes and promises for your life when you are in close proximity to Him.

ACTION

1. What are some tangible ways a man can "fear" God in his choices?

2. Describe the difference between fearing God and being afraid of God.

3. Why does God want you in covenantal alignment with Him?

PRAYER

Jesus, to fear You is to be in alignment with Your will. I discover Your will through the revealed Word. Give me a greater hunger to know Your Word, apply it, and to draw close to You. In Your name, amen.

> Now may the God of peace Himself sanctify you entirely; and may your spirit and soul and body be preserved complete, without blame at the coming of our Lord Jesus Christ.
>
> 1 Thessalonians 5:23

In football, everything is measured by the location of the ball. A first down starts where the ball has been placed. A touchdown happens when the ball crosses the plane of the goal line. A field goal is when the ball goes between the two posts. A reception occurs if the receiver catches the ball. If the receiver bobbles the ball and then drops it, the team heads back to where the ball had been placed at the start of that play. Everything is measured by the presence of and relationship to the football. That reality determines everything that happens in the game, especially the outcome of the game.

Similarly, your relationship to the covenant will determine how much of God you experience, or how little. It will determine how far and how fast you move forward in life. It will determine whether you score or whether you have to keep punting the ball to someone else. Most importantly, it will determine your level of success—

whether you win or lose. Your level of success is all about your connection to the covenant.

You may have accepted Jesus Christ as your personal Savior, and you may have become a son of the King through a spiritual rebirth. But if you are not connected by the relationship of the covenant, through the fear of God, you don't get to fully experience His plans for you. Spiritual success is available through a connection called sanctification, not merely through the legal justification.

ACTION

1. Describe the difference between salvation and sanctification.
2. Define sanctification in your own terms.
3. What is one thing you can do to participate in the process of personal sanctification?

PRAYER

Jesus, my relationship to You through the covenant impacts my ability to live out my purpose as a kingdom man. Make me understand how critical this is so I will pursue it wholly. In Your name, amen.

TWENTY-NINE

> The fear of the LORD prolongs life, but the years of the wicked will be shortened.
>
> Proverbs 10:27

Driving has become a normal way of getting around. But have you ever stopped to think of the power of a car? Without going into the minutia of physics, let me give a fairly simple example. It's been stated that if you crash your car while driving at 65 miles per hour, it is the same force you would face if you drove your car off a twelve-story building.[1]

Now, most of us driving a car on top of a twelve-story building would be extremely careful. Yet many of us casually driving down the road at 65 miles per hour have been known to let our minds wander. The reason we pay more attention on top of the building is that we can see the potential result should we drive off the edge. Resultantly, we take our driving up there seriously. But since we have become so used to driving on highways at 65 miles per hour, many of us don't consider how dangerous it really is. As soon as you take your attention off the road, where it needs to be, a crash can loudly declare, "Game over."

So there are boundaries around the use of a high-powered vehicle. And those boundaries are honored through what we do. In fact, we even tell our kids and grandkids when they are old enough to drive that they are to honor those boundaries. We take driving seriously.

Yet far too many men understand how to take driving seriously but have no clue how to do the same with God. They want the benefits of God without the boundaries that a proper fear and awe of Him create. They treat God like the cop they see in the rearview mirror. He affects what you do when He's in visible proximity—perhaps in church or a small-group setting. But get outside of cultural Christianity, and the foot presses hard on the accelerator once again.

ACTION

1. What are some consequences for failing to fear God?

2. Have you experienced any of these consequences, or similar ones, in your life? If yes, what did you learn?

3. How can we encourage others in our lives to take God more seriously?

Jesus, Your boundaries are there to preserve and protect me. They are not there to cause me harm. Help me to be reminded of this truth so that I will honor the boundaries You have set in place rather than dismiss them. In Your name, amen.

For all have sinned and fall short of the glory of God.

Romans 3:23

What would you say to a basketball player who kept running toward the wrong basket while dribbling the ball? You'd probably tell him to go sit down. As a coach, you wouldn't have time for that.

Thankfully, God doesn't exist in time and He's not bound by linear limitations like we are. He's got all the time in the world, and then some. And He doesn't just kick us off the team for running in the wrong direction. God grasps that none of us is perfect and we all fall short (Romans 3:23). Yet that doesn't make our rebellion any less serious than it is. God's patience doesn't translate into a free pass to keep going with power out of control. God's patience translates into more time for us to grow.

If you have found yourself heading in the wrong direction by what you think, say, or do—turn around. There's no time like the present to get back into alignment with God. God wants you to follow Him. He doesn't want to see you suffer the consequences of living apart from Him and His rule over your life.

1. Describe a moment when you knew you were headed in the wrong direction.

2. What did you choose to do about it?

3. Looking back, are you happy or disappointed with the choices you made?

PRAYER

Jesus, You are full of forgiveness for those who seek You. I want to experience Your forgiveness for anything that I have done that has taken me outside of Your covenantal will for my life. Give me grace and mercy to get back on the right track with You. In Your name, amen.

THIRTY-ONE

"After He had removed him, He raised up David to be their king, concerning whom He also testified and said, 'I have found David the son of Jesse, a man after My heart, who will do all My will.'"

Acts 13:22

King David was a successful warrior even though he grew up herding sheep, skipping rocks, and playing instruments. David didn't attend military school. But he knew the one in charge. And because of that, David won his battles and his wars (see 1 Chronicles 18:1). A critical aspect of David's military leadership and victory came through his awareness of and willingness to seek God's guidance. No other biblical narrative contains more inquiries of God than David's. Each time he asked to know God's will and God's ways, he got an answer.

As a result, David stood strongly positioned to annihilate his enemies and redeem his people from certain death. David, a kingdom man after God's own heart, understood the value of this treasure called guidance. He feared God, which enabled him to follow God more fully.

Life is full of choices. The problem with many of our decisions is that we cannot see what's around the bend.

It's like being on a highway that is twisting and turning and you are unable to see around the next corner. You have to slow down because you don't know where you're going. Life is filled with unknowns. But that's why David prayed a prayer we should all pray as kingdom men: "Make me know Your ways, O LORD; teach me Your paths" (Psalm 25:4). That's not just a sweet verse to say on Sunday. That's a plea for a game plan. It's a cry to know the next call.

ACTION

1. What is your tendency when you reach a point of decision—go to God first or try and figure it out yourself?

2. Was David any less of a man by always going to God for direction?

3. What are some things that cause men to hesitate to go to God for direction?

PRAYER

Jesus, slow down my thinking enough that I have time to discern when I need to go to God for direction. Help me not to get so caught up in being busy that I forget where wisdom comes from. In Your name, amen.

THIRTY-TWO

His soul will abide in prosperity, and his descendants
will inherit the land.

Psalm 25:13

You can have a very big house with two miserable souls
living in it. While the money may have prospered for
the individuals to purchase such a big house, it can't
give wealth to the soul. God says if you fear Him, He
will prosper your soul in such a way that it will impact
everything you engage with. You'll be making wise decisions that will then affect your future success.

A kingdom man doesn't merely focus on the external
things of life without making things better on the in-
side. But Satan has deceived so many of us into spending
money we don't have in order to buy things we don't
need so we can impress people we don't know. But all
we wind up with are bills we can't pay. God's blessings
work toward the well-being of the person. It's not about
the stuff.

God desires to give financial blessing through wise
stewardship of a man. He commands the man to fear Him
and take Him seriously. Then the effects of that obedience ripple out to his family, friends, church, community,

and world. When we align our hearts under Him in a humble reverence for Him, He will guide us as men. He will prosper our souls and enable us to make wise stewardship decisions for ourselves and those around us.

ACTION

1. Why doesn't simply owning stuff bring about personal satisfaction?

2. What are some elements of personal satisfaction that sit outside of the material world?

3. Name one way you honor God through your stewardship of material items.

PRAYER

Jesus, I want to honor You through my use of the material items you have given to me, such as money and tangible goods. Give me greater opportunities to do that. In Your name, amen.

But you are a chosen race, a royal priesthood, a holy nation, a people for God's own possession, so that you may proclaim the excellencies of Him who has called you out of darkness into His marvelous light.

1 Peter 2:9

Legacy is about much more than leaving a name. It's about leaving a lineage of peace, strength, and spiritual impact. The treasures of the covenant don't just belong to you. When you apply and use the key to spiritual success, you are also setting up your descendants for their own spiritual achievements.

God wants to bless you with guidance. He wants to prosper your soul. And He wants to use you to leave a legacy. All He's waiting on in order to do those three things is for you to align your life under Him. When you begin to take Him and His Word seriously on a consistent basis, He will take you to your promised land.

Now, you may have made mistakes along the way. You may have lost time. But if you will humble yourself beneath God right now, He can make it so that you do not waste the rest of your life. I want to encourage you to let God do His work. Let Him lead you, even if it looks like you might be going backward for some time. There are seasons in life when we need to address and untangle the messes we find ourselves in before we can develop and mature enough to handle the successes up ahead. God has a plan for you. He has a destiny for you. But the road to that destiny requires development first.

ACTION

1. What does it look like to take God's Word seriously on a consistent basis?

2. Do you ever feel like you are wasting your life? Why or why not?

3. What are some hesitations you have about developing spiritually?

PRAYER

Jesus, help me to mature and develop spiritually by learning how to take Your word seriously and apply it to my daily choices. Show me what I need to do in order to better serve You. In Your name, amen.

THIRTY-FOUR

For bodily discipline is only of little profit, but godliness is profitable for all things, since it holds promise for the present life and also for the life to come.

1 Timothy 4:8

One of the greatest challenges in our culture is the sheer difficulty of calling men to unleash their biblical manhood. It seems that simply taking responsibility for your thoughts and actions has become a lost art. We might be facing a worldwide plague of personal irresponsibility and entitlement. And that just doesn't cut it in the long run.

Imagine if a football coach drafted a star running back with all the potential in the world. He had speed. Moves. Balance. Intuition to read the opposition. All of that and more. On paper, he was amazing. But when he showed up to practice, he just sat down the whole time.

If the coach told him to get on the field to practice, he'd just shrug it off and say he didn't feel like it. Or that he was busy. Or any other excuse that came to mind. Then, on game day, when he failed to make the plays or score the points and the coach asked him why he didn't accomplish the goals of the game, he just blamed the opposition. Or, worse yet, he blamed his teammates.

This player wouldn't last long on this team, regardless of his stats, strength, and size when they drafted him. Unleashing a powerful running back requires more than stats and natural ability. It requires intentionality, practice, and responsibility. Unleashing biblical manhood requires no less.

ACTION

1. What would the common response be to the coach who cut the player that didn't exert himself or practice?

2. Why do we often judge God when He chooses not to participate in or bless the lives of men who do not actively pursue Him?

3. Describe what personal spiritual responsibility means to you.

PRAYER

Jesus, applying spiritual responsibility in my life requires effort and a heart to seek You in all I do. Help me to break free from the bonds of laziness in order to experience You more fully. In Your name, amen.

When Jesus saw him lying there, and knew that he had already been a long time in that condition, He said to him, "Do you wish to get well?"

John 5:6

To unleash the full potential of who you are as a kingdom man, you'll need to first make sure you're up for the challenge. Manning up starts by standing up. If you do not take the divinely ordained responsibility that God has given to you, and every man, by virtue of His created purpose when He made you, then you are wasting your life. Even with fineries decorating your home, office, or social media sites—an irresponsible man is no kingdom man at all.

Healing and empowerment are not a one-way gift bestowed with a magic wand. To be unleashed in your fullest potential requires your desire, responsibility, and focus. That's why Jesus would often ask the question "Do you want to be made well?" He didn't just walk around tapping people on the head, bestowing health and power on whomever was near. Rather, Jesus would ask if the person was willing to be made whole. He did this because if he or she was not willing, He couldn't help them.

Wholeness and strength have to come from within. You don't light a candle by putting a flame to the outer wax. You have to light the wick.

You also don't place a candle under direct sunlight, not if you don't want to waste it. But far too many men are content with being like the flicker of a candle under the noonday sun. Unnoticed. Leaving no impact. Making no mark on a world that desperately needs kingdom men.

ACTION

1. Do you wish to get well?

2. How have you expressed this wish to Jesus?

3. What improvements in your life has Jesus been free to make over the last year?

PRAYER

Jesus, I want to be whole and healed of anything that keeps me from fully living out my purpose in Your kingdom plan. Help me to overcome my addictions and propensities that draw me away from You. In Your name, amen.

For the love of money is a root of all sorts of evil, and some by longing for it have wandered away from the faith and pierced themselves with many griefs.

1 Timothy 6:10

Most men think money is the secret to satisfaction. They think that happiness equates to how much money you've got at your disposal. But happiness has nothing to do with money. Money isn't about to solve your problems. In fact, oftentimes the problems in people's lives escalate as money increases—not the other way around.

There are many things money can't buy. Money can't buy health. It can't buy relational harmony. It can't buy respect, honor, character, or esteem. When things go south in any of those areas and others, and money is all you've got working for you, you'll find out the real value of money. You'll quickly learn that money isn't all it's cracked up to be. There's so much more that really matters. But it's very easy to forget that.

As a result, men frequently pray for stuff when God wants to give them more than stuff. He wants to give significance, strength, stability, and identity. All the stuff in the world doesn't mean a hill of beans if you are so broken, empty, or alone that you cannot enjoy it and you don't have anyone with whom to enjoy it. Stuff never made a man smile the way that satisfaction, purpose, and even service do. Yet even so, we've got a world focused on stuff.

ACTION

1. Why do you think money does not satisfy in the way we hope it will?
2. Have you ever purchased anything only to experience buyer's remorse, and if so, what did you learn?
3. What step can you take to distance yourself from the love of money this week?

PRAYER

Jesus, free me from the love of money. I do not want money to become a stranglehold that pins me down. Show me the things in this life that bring true satisfaction and joy. In Your name, amen.

THIRTY-SEVEN

So that at the name of Jesus every knee will bow, of those
who are in heaven and on earth and under the earth.

Philippians 2:10

In the Bible, names matter. Names have meanings. Names
are never mere nomenclature. People weren't named because it sounded nice, or their parents were copying a ce-
lebrity somewhere, or their mom suggested it—*strongly*.
Names carried weight and character and were often tied
to the future. That's why, throughout Scripture, when
God was about to do something new in a place or with
a person, He would often change the name.

Abram became Abraham.

Jacob became Israel.

Simon became Peter.

Saul became Paul.

All through the Bible, God is switching around names
because He's switching up identities or purposes tied
to His kingdom roles. A person was given a new name
designed to fit the reputation or character of his or her
new path. Names held power tied to purpose.

The name of Jesus, of course, held—and holds—the power above all power.

It's time to own your life through a proper understanding and use of the power of the name of Jesus. It's time to take charge of who you are by identifying with Him. Stop letting other people's thoughts, words, or actions drive you down. There is power in the name of Jesus, even when there's no money on the table. Because in His name, you can get up and send your opposition flying while unleashing your full potential.

ACTION

1. What does your name mean?

2. Why do you think God wanted you to have that name?

3. Have you lived up to your name? If not, what do you need to do to live up to its meaning?

PRAYER

Jesus, give me a greater understanding and awareness of what my purpose is in life so that I can fulfill the plans You have for me. Help me to identify my calling and live up to the name You have chosen for me on this journey. In Your name, amen.

THIRTY-EIGHT

For whatever is born of God overcomes the world; and this is the victory that has overcome the world—our faith.

1 John 5:4

Perhaps you didn't have a good beginning upon which to build. Maybe your parents fought or divorced early on. Maybe you didn't come from a nice neighborhood or a school system whose funding indicated that they took your future seriously. Maybe you had to raise yourself because your mom worked three jobs. Or maybe you lived in the suburbs, but you were abused, neglected, or pacified with stuff. You were kept busy to keep you away from any real relationship at home. Whatever the case, where you start has nothing to do with where you are going. Jesus started out in an obscure town named Nazareth, after all.

Since Jesus came from this no-name place, He can meet any man in any place at any time, even when your life seems worthless. He can turn it around and set you on your feet, if you will just look to Jesus from Nazareth. Look to the Jesus from no hope, no opportunity, and no way out—let alone up.

The truth of this reality strips men of any excuses they might have claimed, like "If it weren't for him," or "If it weren't for them," or "If it weren't for that circumstance, or my background, or my limitations." All that is real, yes, but in the name of Jesus Christ, the one from *Nazareth*, you don't need to be whining anymore. You can get up. You can walk. You can be responsible. You are no longer to see yourself as a victim. Your relationship with Jesus Christ makes you an overcomer (1 John 5:1–4).

ACTION

1. What is one thing from your past that you need to overcome or let go of so you can move forward?

2. What are you willing to do in order to stop blaming that situation or person and move on?

3. Why do you think Jesus wants you to stop the blame game?

PRAYER

Jesus, the things that have happened to me in my past were allowed by You. I trust that You had a plan for them. Show me how I can let go of the pain of the past in order to be set free from a cycle of blame. In Your name, amen.

THIRTY-NINE

And they overcame him because of the blood of the Lamb and because of the word of their testimony, and they did not love their life even when faced with death.

Revelation 12:11

Suddenly. It's a word you'll hear often in the Bible. One thing you need to understand as you dive deeper into this concept of unleashing biblical manhood is that God doesn't need time. He can do whatever He wants whenever He wants to. He's just waiting for you to look to Him in order to receive a supernatural infusion of His power. The moment you are ready, God is too. When God wants to move, He can move faster than an X-15 fighter tearing across the sky at Mach 6.

God wants you whole and strong not just for you. He wants those in your circle of influence to be spiritually healthy and mature too. If all you are doing is participating in church or attending a small group or throwing God a prayer here or there, you are not demonstrating to others who God has created you to be.

If and when God transforms any aspect of your life (emotions, addictions, relationships, and more), you've got to make it known. You've got to share this truth with others. Don't be ashamed. Don't be shy. God has given you your testimony for a reason. Don't miss the purpose of the miracle, which is to draw others toward their miracles as quickly as God chooses.

ACTION

1. Have you ever shared your testimony publicly, and if so, what was the result?

2. Why is it important to tell others what Jesus has done for you?

3. Have you been encouraged by someone else's testimony, and if so, how did that impact your life?

PRAYER

Jesus, give me a greater level of boldness to share the things You have done in my life with others. I want to be someone who encourages others through the telling of the impact You have made both in and through me. In Your name, amen.

And do not be conformed to this world, but be transformed by the renewing of your mind, so that you may prove what the will of God is, that which is good and acceptable and perfect.

Romans 12:2

A POW is a prisoner of war—a person who has been captured by the enemy and is held hostage in the context of a conflict. The opposing forces control the prisoner's living conditions, activities, and movements. Many men live like POWs, but rather than being prisoners of war, they're prisoners of addictive behavior. They have been captured by the enemy, and there appears to be no way of escape.

They feel trapped in situations and circumstances that the world labels as addiction. Drugs, sex, pornography, alcohol, relationships, negative self-talk, work, food, gambling, spending—these things can become the go-to coping mechanisms for life's pain, disappointments, and boredom. When an action or activity begins to influence you more than you influence it, it can leave you feeling trapped—as if there is no way out.

Overcoming addictions—whether these are addictions to work, approval, physique, status, drugs, alcohol, or something else—begins with identifying the root of the problem and addressing it in your mind. Maybe you're dealing with loneliness or depression or past trauma or something else. Whatever is leading you to addiction, these issues must be addressed for you to fully unleash your biblical manhood as a kingdom man. If you don't address those issues, then addictions will leave their negative impacts through broken relationships, broken bodies, broken dreams, and destroyed lives. It is time to be set free from the symptoms of wrong thinking. It's up to you to get started on the path to wholeness and victorious kingdom living.

ACTION

1. What is the root of one of the prominent struggles or addictions you face or have faced?

2. What are some ways the root can be extracted or healed in your life?

3. What happens if you seek to treat symptoms of a stronghold rather than the root?

Jesus, reveal to me the root at the heart of the struggles I face and the strongholds that seek to consume me. Show me how to address the root and heal from whatever I need to be healed from in order to experience the freedom of Your love. In Your name, amen.

FORTY-ONE

> "I am the vine, you are the branches; he who abides in Me and I in him, he bears much fruit, for apart from Me you can do nothing."
>
> John 15:5

You are free to get over whatever it is that has gripped you as soon as you decide to do just that. How long you've been bound doesn't matter. How deep the addiction runs doesn't matter. You can get up. You can get over the obstacles that keep you down.

God frequently uses broken people to accomplish His kingdom agenda on earth. Time after time in Scripture, we read about the broken people God raised up in a powerful way. He used Moses, a murderer, to deliver the Hebrew slaves. He used Jacob, a liar and a trickster, to fulfill His promise to Abraham. He even used Peter after his denial, Solomon after his idolatry, and Samson after his multiple failures. If God redeemed their lives, He can redeem your life too.

Brokenness should never keep you bound. A broken past should never limit a bright future. Rather, it should release you into a greater life of purpose through what you have learned, because a truly broken person understands the reality of John 15:5, where Jesus says, "Apart from Me you can do nothing." A broken man who has learned both surrender to and dependence on God is a force to be reckoned with.

ACTION

1. What is your vision for how you want God to use you in the future?
2. How can you participate in the fulfillment of this vision?
3. What hesitations do you have about participating?

PRAYER

Jesus, show me Your plans for me and how You want to go about bringing these plans to fruition. Help me to understand Your purpose for my life so that I can participate with You in living it out. In Your name, amen.

FORTY-TWO

Be of sober spirit, be on the alert. Your adversary, the devil, prowls around like a roaring lion, seeking someone to devour.

1 Peter 5:8

God looks at your future, while the enemy tries to keep you in your past. God says, "You can, in spite of what has been done!" The enemy says, "You can't, because of what you have done!" God will never define you by your past issues, but the enemy will try to confine you by them. Whether it is the good, bad, or ugly that has dominated your life up until now, it is Satan's goal to keep you chained there.

Never let your yesterday keep you from your tomorrow. Learn from yesterday, but don't live in it. Your victory comes through learning and then applying what you've learned. Unleashing biblical manhood starts with your thoughts.

Always remember that Satan's number one strategy to keep you in unhealthy addictive cycles is to mess with your mind. He likes to plant thoughts in your mind, repeating them over and over until you start to think they are your own thoughts. When Satan told Eve she would be like God if she ate of the fruit, whose thought was that? Was that Eve's thought? No. That thought came straight from Satan himself. In fact, he'd had the same thought before, as we read in Isaiah 14:14: "I will make myself like the Most High." It was Satan's thought, but he planted it in Eve's mind. Be mindful of the devil. Don't let him have free rein in your mind.

ACTION

1. In what ways do you allow your past to stop you from living out a wonderful future?

2. Is it possible for a person to judge himself when God has already given grace?

3. What does judging yourself accomplish?

PRAYER

Jesus, free me from the chains of my past so that I can be released to pursue the pathway to living as a victorious kingdom man. You give me hope for my future, and I praise You for it. In Your name, amen.

FORTY-THREE

"You are of your father the devil, and you want to do the desires of your father. He was a murderer from the beginning, and does not stand in the truth because there is no truth in him. Whenever he speaks a lie, he speaks from his own nature, for he is a liar and the father of lies."

John 8:44

When you tell yourself, *I can't overcome this addiction*, whose thought is that? Or when you think, *I have to have this drink*, whose thought is that? Or when you entertain such thoughts as *I am nothing. I have no value. I don't have power over my emotions of lust or anger*, who is doing the talking? We know these thoughts come from Satan because they are all lies, and he is the father of lies (John 8:44).

Satan makes quick work of planting and directing thoughts. But his thoughts do not have to have the last word. You have the power to control your own thoughts. How should you respond to Satan's thoughts? The same way Jesus did when Peter tried to keep Him from going to the cross. Peter told Jesus, "God forbid it, Lord! This shall never happen to You."

To which Jesus replied, "Get behind Me, Satan!" (Matthew 16:22–23).

The words came from Peter, but the thoughts came from Satan. When Satan gets into your mind, he gets into your actions. The key to overcoming addictive behavior is to take your thoughts captive.

ACTION

1. How can a believer discern between thoughts planted by Satan and his own thoughts?
2. Do you make discernment an active part of your life? If not, will you consider doing so?
3. What do you think are some of Satan's goals in planting thoughts in Christians' minds?

PRAYER

Jesus, give me greater discernment to be able to cut through the lies of Satan and identify Your truth. Help me not to fall into the trap of lies and deception. In Your name, amen.

FORTY-FOUR

> But I am afraid that, as the serpent deceived Eve by his craftiness, your minds will be led astray from the simplicity and purity of devotion to Christ.
>
> 2 Corinthians 11:3

Scripture tells us that as a man *thinks*, so that man *is* (Proverbs 23:7). This passage is the foundation for overcoming all addictive behavior. Memorize that verse. Understand its impact on all you do in life. Your addiction doesn't stem from the item or vice itself. It stems from your thoughts. Your addiction is rooted, and fed, in your mind. Once Satan plants thoughts in your mind and you allow them to continue—even helping them to grow through your actions or inaction—those thoughts then transfer biologically and physiologically to your emotions.

Satan seeks to capture your thoughts because they are what will trigger your emotions, which in turn influence your actions. Thus, addictions are prolonged through emotional manipulations. The alcoholism, drug abuse, endless spending, excessive working, pornography viewing, ongoing masturbation, or obsession with power is a reaction to an emotion that has affected your body's cravings and needs. Understanding the physiological impact of your thoughts on your emotions, and ultimately on your body, helps to underscore where the battle for your freedom exists. It is entirely in your thoughts.

Gain mastery of your thoughts and you will master your emotions. Master your emotions and you will overcome any addiction or stronghold that holds you hostage.

ACTION

1. Describe the link between a man's thoughts and his emotions.

2. Why do you think Satan likes to go after a man's thoughts—what emotional response is he seeking to trigger?

3. What practice can you put in place to help you identify when Satan is targeting your thoughts with his deception?

PRAYER

Jesus, I want to master my emotions so that my emotions no longer master and drive me where they want me to go. Help me to capture my thoughts and hold them up to Your standard and Your truth so that I do not succumb to the enemy's schemes. In Your name, amen.

FORTY-FIVE

> We are destroying speculations and every lofty thing raised up against the knowledge of God, and we are taking every thought captive to the obedience of Christ.
>
> 2 Corinthians 10:5

One reason strongholds are so powerful is that they are so entrenched. They become entrenched when Satan gets you to buy into the lie that your situation is hopeless. His goal is to get you to believe that by nature you are a drug addict or a manipulator or a negative person, that you are controlled by fear or shame, that nothing will ever change, and so on. Once you give in to and adopt this line of thinking, the entrenched fortresses become difficult to remove. Your behavior deteriorates even more because we always act according to who we believe we are.

The only solution is to tear down these fortresses by "taking every thought captive to the obedience of Christ" (2 Corinthians 10:5). Reprogram your mind and release yourself from captivity. This is how you unleash your full potential and free yourself up to then help other men rise to do the same.

The solution is twofold but straightforward. First, identify Christ's thoughts on a matter, and secondly, align your own thinking under the rule of His truth. The truth, then, will set you free (John 8:32).

ACTION

1. How has a sense of hopelessness impacted your life or decisions either recently or in the past?
2. According to God's Word, is there ever a time to lack hope?
3. What area in your life needs a boost in hope?

PRAYER

Jesus, give me hope. Renew my hope in Your saving power. Restore my hope in Your plan. Let me see things and experience things that will expand my hopefulness in a new way. In Your name, amen.

FORTY-SIX

But I say, walk by the Spirit, and you will not carry out
the desire of the flesh.

Galatians 5:16

One of the most important lessons to learn in your development as a kingdom man is that your own choices
are what lead to a dire state of distress in your life. You
must remove blame from your vocabulary. God allows
the consequences to play out because He wants you to
learn from your sins and discover how to control your
emotions.

I'm sure you've watched football or another sport
where the emotions get out of hand. It could be a playoff
game where everything is on the line. And then, because
of heated emotions, one player shoves another and the
one who was shoved punches back. Because the first
shove wasn't seen, the player who is penalized is the one
who responded. Games have been lost this way. No matter what has happened to you, do not make it worse with
your response. Keep your eye on the true goal at hand.

One of the goals God has in either allowing or creating
a crisis in your life is to force your return to Him. When
your departure leads to living out of alignment with His

will, God will often permit difficulties to happen, which will get you back on track.

ACTION

1. Why is it important to accept responsibility for the difficulties you face?
2. What do blame and regret prevent, or possibly lead to, in a person's life?
3. What is one way to overcome feelings of blame and hurt from the past?

PRAYER

Jesus, enable me to keep my eye on the overarching goal. Help me to see how hard I have worked to get here so that I do not lose it all through a wrong emotional response to difficulties in my life. In Your name, amen.

FORTY-SEVEN

> Let all bitterness and wrath and anger and clamor and slander be put away from you, along with all malice. Be kind to one another, tender-hearted, forgiving each other, just as God in Christ also has forgiven you.
>
> Ephesians 4:31–32

God knows what you need most in the midst of your struggle and pain. Thus, He often chooses not to answer our questions of "why" when we ask them. Maybe it is because He has already answered and we just didn't like the answer or pay attention. Or it could be that He wants to shift our focus off of yesterday and direct it toward tomorrow. Whatever the reason, you must remember that while there are times that warrant asking God "why"—and you always have a right to ask—you must never demand an answer.

Another thing to keep in mind is that it is not wise to allow the *why* to become a way of life. If you do, you could wind up stuck in a victim mind-set, which only pins you down. Far too many men forfeit a greater future because they remain chained to the hurts of the past. Now, I understand that the things that happened back then may have been rough. They may have been unfair.

But you can't change the past. No one can. You need to stop allowing your past to dominate your present and consequently destroy your future. Let it go, get up, and move on. A kingdom man entertains a question or two, from himself or those under his care, but then he goes forward to search for the solution.

ACTION

1. Is there someone or multiple people you need to forgive?
2. Is there anything preventing you from forgiving them, and if so, what is it?
3. Why is it important to forgive those who have wronged us?

PRAYER

Jesus, I know that I ask why from time to time, but You are not required to give me an answer. I want to trust You more fully than I do. Help me to focus on You rather than trying to figure things out for myself. In Your name, amen.

FORTY-EIGHT

"The Lord is the one who goes ahead of you; He will be with you. He will not fail you or forsake you. Do not fear or be dismayed."

Deuteronomy 31:8

When it comes to God and His plans for your life, your lineage, standing, and position don't matter. All that matters is who goes with you. It's a simple spiritual point but one we often gloss over to our own detriment. The key to accomplishing any impossible task is the presence of the Lord with you. It doesn't depend on your expertise or lack thereof. It doesn't even depend on your strength. Your strategy is no match for God's, so you might as well table it and follow Him. Spiritual success in spiritual war depends entirely upon spiritual solutions. Spiritual solutions take place if, and when, God goes before you or with you. That determines your outcome.

God either needs to go before you or with you to overcome the enemy at hand. His presence is your power. His wisdom secures your win. And remember, it's always okay to ask for confirmation on something as important as that. Valiant warriors in God's kingdom know their own limits. Just like Gideon set out the fleece to be sure he was hearing from God correctly, you can ask God for your own signs of confirmation. As long as what you believe He is telling you does not contradict His own Word, Scripture, you are free to move forward based on His confirming His path for you.

ACTION

1. Why is it important to let go of your own strategies in order to embrace God's?
2. What is one thing that holds you back from doing that?
3. Describe the difference between spiritual solutions and physical solutions to life's challenges.

PRAYER

Jesus, help me to pause and truly step back from trying to run my own show. I don't want to get in the way of what You are doing. Show me how to get a better idea of Your strategies for overcoming spiritual obstacles in my life. In Your name, amen.

FORTY-NINE

> "For whoever has, to him more shall be given, and he will have an abundance; but whoever does not have, even what he has shall be taken away from him."
>
> Matthew 13:12

God desires to raise you up to serve Him in a mighty conquest to advance His kingdom agenda. But prior to taking you there, He asks you to be obedient with what He has called you to do right now. Matthew 13:12 summarizes this principle of demonstrating faithfulness with where you are before God gives you more responsibility in His kingdom.

Faithfulness with what you have right now and right where you are is always the first step toward further use in God's kingdom. We saw this in the life of Shamgar in *Kingdom Man* (read Shamgar's story in Judges 3:31). God wants to see if you are willing to follow Him right where you are. He wants to know what you are willing to do right now at your home—with your family and friends and even in your neighborhood and church. Don't waste your time on visions of grandeur if you are not willing to begin by achieving the small victories that are yours to grab first.

Let God use you where you are. Let Him see your willingness to follow Him. As He does, He will make your next move clear to You. You don't need to figure out how to get to the dreams He has placed in your soul. You just need to be faithful with each step in front of you right now.

ACTION

1. What is one way you can be obedient with what God has given you right now to serve Him?
2. Have you witnessed God expand His use of you over time?
3. Why is it easy to get frustrated when dreams and visions do not quickly come to pass?

PRAYER

Jesus, I don't want to waste my life swinging for the fences when You are asking me to get on first base first. Help me to be obedient where I am right now. I trust that You will take me down the path of greatest impact. In Your name, amen.

> "Have I not commanded you? Be strong and courageous!
> Do not tremble or be dismayed, for the Lord your God is
> with you wherever you go."
>
> Joshua 1:9

While God provides pockets of peace in moments of uncertainty, our humanity leaves us vulnerable to ongoing emotional changes based on what we've been tasked with. Obedience as a kingdom man isn't always couched in calm. Sometimes that obedience takes place in a mixture of emotions. Courage does not mean the absence of fear. Courage means right actions taken in spite of fear's presence.

There's nothing courageous about doing something you know will succeed without any opposition. Courage occurs when you rise up to do the task that looks impossible.

I understand that it can be frustrating when circumstances don't appear to be in your favor. Or during those times when you want to be the person you know you can be but things haven't fallen in line. It can take a toll on anyone's patience when dreams rise up within but life seems to be solely about surviving each day. You know you were made for more. You know you can accomplish more. But you feel stuck. But remember that even though waiting can be frustrating, when God decides to move He can shift the landscape overnight. I've seen Him do it in my own life many times. I've also seen Him do it for others. When God is ready, it doesn't take long. He can turn a servant in a field into a Baal fighter leading the charge to freedom for a whole nation. He did it for Gideon, and He can do it for you.

ACTION

1. Describe the difference between spiritual courage based on God's definition and humanity's courage based on cultural norms?

2. Why does it take courage to follow God?

3. Do other people always get to witness someone's courageous acts? Why or why not?

PRAYER

Jesus, give me greater courage to follow You. I want to be used by You for advancing Your kingdom agenda on this earth. Help me to have the wisdom needed to do just that. In Your name, amen.

> "For the LORD your God is the one who goes with you, to fight for you against your enemies, to save you."
>
> Deuteronomy 20:4

Part of rising up as a kingdom man involves doing what God says even when it doesn't make sense. As long as the way you think God is leading you doesn't contradict His revealed principles in His Word, and you have received confirmation from Him to get going, you are to go. Your response to His leading often plays a larger role in the outcome than the strategy itself. When God is ready to move, it doesn't matter how big your enemy is. It doesn't matter how entrenched the opposition is or how shattered your world is. Nothing and no one can override God when He sets His mind on victory.

Kingdom men exist today in the midst of a pagan nation, on many levels. We are sorely outnumbered as disciples in the body of Christ. The secular world has not only abandoned God, but it has taken up the offensive against the one true God. It is oppressing the church and the truth of Scripture in many ways. This is our cultural reality whether we like it or not. We can pretend it doesn't exist, but that won't change what we are facing.

It doesn't take millions to take ground back for Christ. It only takes a few committed kingdom men. We are to rise up and do what God has called each of us to do so that we might advance His kingdom agenda on earth.

ACTION

1. Have you ever done what God told you to do when it didn't make sense? If so, what was the result?

2. In what ways does the culture oppress Christian values in our land?

3. What is the greatest thing you have ever accomplished for God's kingdom?

PRAYER

Jesus, the need to rise up as kingdom men is here. I raise my voice in obedience to Your calling. I offer myself to You as a kingdom warrior to advance Your cause in our land and around the world. In Your name, amen.

FIFTY-TWO

Being diligent to preserve the unity of the Spirit in the bond of peace.

Ephesians 4:3

The reason we haven't solved the race problem in America after hundreds of years is that people apart from God are trying to create unity, while people under God who already have unity are not living out the unity we possess. Unless kingdom-minded Christians significantly enter the fray and become leaders in resolving the race crisis, we will be hopelessly deadlocked in a sea of relativity, resulting in restating more questions rather than providing permanent answers. It's only when believers step out and put biblical theology concerning issues such as injustice, unity, and reconciliation on display—not just through words—that we can set a different tone and create a divine reset.

Until we see ourselves, and each other, as God sees us and respond by intentionally embracing His call of oneness, we will forever, like the cracked Liberty Bell, ring flat in a world that longs to hear the liberating cadence of truth.

ACTION

1. In what ways do you intentionally seek out cross-racial interaction and impact?

2. Why is it important to be intentional about racial unity?

3. What are some hindrances to being intentional about racial unity?

PRAYER

Jesus, show me how I can be intentional about seeking to preserve racial unity in the body of Christ. I want to be a difference-maker in a world that is increasingly more divided each day and each decade. In Your name, amen.

FIFTY-THREE

> Clouds and thick darkness surround Him; righteousness
> and justice are the foundation of His throne.
>
> Psalm 97:2

God has been known to allow chaos in order to create
in His people a heartfelt call to Him for help. When we
appeal to Him according to His kingdom rule, He can
then reintroduce himself into the scenario and usher in
the healing we so desperately need. Sometimes it takes
a mess to make a miracle.

Everyone knows what it's like to suffer for a long time
from stomach pains and then throw up and feel better
relatively quickly. The throwing up is a messy situation,
but the reason you feel better afterward is that you have
purged the toxins.

There are a lot of toxins in our culture. We have toxins
of injustice, toxins of racism, and toxins of hate. We have
a multiplicity of toxins coagulating in the same space
at the same time. But if we miss the reality that God
has allowed disorder to bring about a correction and a
cleaning, then we will just move from one symptom to
another symptom. We will miss the opportunity to address the root that has produced the fruit that has led

to the confusion of hopelessness on display. The root of the problems we face in our nation today are clearly spiritual. It's only when we identify and understand the spiritual components that we are able to translate them to the pragmatic realities of the cultural crisis at hand.

ACTION

1. What is at the root of racial and class division in our culture?
2. What would you suggest could be done to bring about healing and unity?
3. Why does Satan seek to divide people, especially in the body of Christ?

PRAYER

Jesus, help us as a global body of Christ to seek unity in all we do. Humble us so that we do not live in the sins of pride and self-righteousness, which produce division. In Your name, amen.

FIFTY-FOUR

Righteousness and justice are the foundation of Your throne; lovingkindness and truth go before You.

Psalm 89:14

Righteousness and justice are not a seesaw to go up and down on. Rather, these are twins joined at the hip. You don't skip justice and call for righteousness. Likewise, you don't skip righteousness in the name of justice.

Righteousness is the moral standard of right and wrong to which God holds people accountable based on His divine standard. *Justice* is the equitable and impartial application of God's moral law in society.

God desires and requires His kingdom men to juxtapose both in our daily lives. God wants to protect the life of the unborn in the womb, but He also wants to see justice for life once born to the tomb. In other words, God wants a whole-life agenda and not a term agenda. But unfortunately, all lives aren't valued the same way in our country right now, even though they ought to be because every person is created in the image of Almighty God.

ACTION

1. Describe in your own words the difference between righteousness and justice.
2. Which do you emphasize more?
3. Why do you think it's easy to emphasize one area over the other?

PRAYER

Jesus, help me to live according to the principles of both righteousness and justice. Show me what areas I need to grow in so that I reflect both equally. In Your name, amen.

FIFTY-FIVE

> Now I exhort you, brethren, by the name of our Lord Jesus Christ, that you all agree and that there be no divisions among you, but that you be made complete in the same mind and in the same judgment.
>
> 1 Corinthians 1:10

Unity isn't just about getting along; it's about getting things done. We'll never experience a movement of kingdom men rising in our nation until we have kingdom men relating to each other in the body of Christ in an authentic, mutually honoring manner.

Racial reconciliation isn't about playing a video of an ethnic preacher to your white church on Sunday, or vice versa, or even reading *White Fragility* or *Oneness Embraced* and posting online that you did so. While those things are good, they—in and of themselves—are not unity. Unity takes place when people join together with oneness of purpose. It is working together in harmony toward a shared vision and goal. Unity involves doing justice together, not just talking about it.

Unity is not uniformity either. Nor is it sameness. Just as the Godhead is made up of three distinct persons— the Father, the Son, and the Holy Spirit—each unique in personhood and yet at the same time one in essence, unity reflects a oneness that does not negate individuality.

Unity does not mean everyone needs to be like everyone else. God's creative variety is replete, displaying itself through a humanity crafted in different shapes, colors, and styles. Each of us, in one way or another, is unique.

Unity occurs when we combine our unique strengths and skills as we head toward a common goal. It is the sense that the thing we are gathered for and moving toward is bigger than our individual preferences. Our common goal is ushering in the manifestation of God's overarching kingdom rule on earth.

ACTION

1. What are some hindrances to biblical unity in our culture?
2. Can you identify a way to overcome any of these hindrances personally?
3. What would it look like for you to increase your intentionality in pursuing unity?

PRAYER

Jesus, help me know what it would take for me to increase my intentionality in pursuing unity. Help me to put these practices and plans into action. In Your name, amen.

FIFTY-SIX

> "By this all men will know that you are My disciples, if you have love for one another."
>
> John 13:35

Just hours before He laid down His life for us, Jesus Christ placed a tremendous emphasis on His desire for us to be one as His followers. This isn't something He is asking us to do only during "Unity Month" or on "Cross-Cultural Sunday." This is a mandate from our Commander in Chief that we be *one* with Him (vertically) and, as a result, *one* with each other (horizontally).

Another benefit of living a life of unity as kingdom men is that, in doing so, we are rising up to let the world know about the King under whom we serve. Getting along in authentic unity brings glory to God by allowing us to experience God's response of fully manifesting His glory in history. All of the prayers, preaching, worship, and Bible studies in the world can never bring about the fullest possible manifestation of God's presence like functioning in a spirit of unity in the body of Christ can (see John 17:1–26).

This is precisely why the subject was the core of Jesus' high priestly prayer. It was the core because it reveals

God's glory unlike anything else. It does this while at the same time revealing an authentic connection between one another in the body of Christ, which serves as a testimony of our connection with Christ.

ACTION

1. What are some benefits of living in unity in the body of Christ?

2. What are some disadvantages when the body of Christ does not live in unity?

3. Do you think we are experiencing more benefits or more disadvantages in our culture?

PRAYER

Jesus, enable me to be an instrument of unity to those around me in all I do and say. Give me relationships that will allow me to create greater emphasis on unity in my life. In Your name, amen.

FIFTY-SEVEN

> The idols of the nations are but silver and gold, the work of man's hands. They have mouths, but they do not speak; they have eyes, but they do not see; they have ears, but they do not hear, nor is there any breath at all in their mouths. Those who make them will be like them, yes, everyone who trusts in them.
>
> Psalm 135:15–18

Soldiers in a war don't care about the color of the person next to them, as long as they are shooting in the same direction. When individuals or communities face challenging circumstances, a unified approach to the solutions at hand must take place. *United we stand, divided we fall* is not just a catchphrase to post on social media or put on the bumper of your car. It's truth. Yet, as we are seeing through the cultural events unfolding more and more these days, without this truth and these values passed down to the next generations, we will face unending chaos and distress.

When men fail to transfer the faith, we wind up with a generation of young people who do not know the Lord, His heart, or His rule. Any culture disintegrates when worship turns away from God and toward idols. The idols might be money, power, prestige, or even education—but whatever it is, an idol holds no candle to God. It cannot save you when you need it most.

In addition, if and when God is no longer worshiped, God will do what He always did in Scripture and throughout history. He will back off. He will remove himself from the consequences brought on by the systematic marginalization of His presence.

ACTION

1. What are the results of God disengaging from culture?
2. Why would God choose to disengage from members of the body of Christ?
3. What areas in our culture are experiencing the greatest division?

PRAYER

Jesus, I do not want to be lured into loving idols. Keep me from temptation. Help me to avoid the traps and snares of Satan. Show me the way out so that I can always function with Your full presence. In Your name, amen.

FIFTY-EIGHT

To the pure, all things are pure; but to those who are defiled and unbelieving, nothing is pure, but both their mind and their conscience are defiled.

Titus 1:15

When you remove conscience from a society, everyone is at risk. When people no longer care about themselves or anyone else, the culture is in jeopardy. The further you move away from God, the further you move away from conscience. The further you move away from conscience, the more dangerous things become. What's more, there is no politician in the world who can impose a law to legislate morality. The issues we face in our nation are ethical, moral, and spiritual at their core. This is because when you leave God and His values out of the dialogue and solutions, you create chaos.

Transferring kingdom values must take place on a regular basis through reminders and authentic conversations. It's not done only through seminars, books, or radio broadcasts. Those things are good, but they are supplemental. The transferring of kingdom values, as clearly outlined in Scripture, takes place person to person and heart to heart.

1. When did you first realize our society no longer had a godly conscience?
2. Is there any practical way to seek to reinsert a godly conscience into the society?
3. What are some dangers we are facing as a nation due to this lack of a moral compass?

PRAYER

Jesus, please reinsert yourself into our culture through the people who seek Your name. Show us what we need to do to rise up collectively and leave an impact for good. In Your name, amen.

FIFTY-NINE

Let the word of Christ richly dwell within you, with all wisdom teaching and admonishing one another with psalms and hymns and spiritual songs, singing with thankfulness in your hearts to God.

Colossians 3:16

Transferring kingdom principles doesn't only happen in small-group settings when we share about past adventures, although that is important. Life lessons often must be experienced by the individuals themselves in order to root deeply.

Discipleship doesn't take place only through discourse. It comes through relationship, partnering, and doing life together. Yet it seems that we often get so focused on the pro forma group studies, weekly meetings, or programs that we have forgotten this truth. We have forgotten what actually accomplishes the outcomes we desire and so desperately need. After all, reading through the "Red Sea Miracle in Seven Weeks" study can only go so far.

Unfortunately, too often we expect those we influence—whether men we disciple, our adult children, teens, or those we serve with who are younger in the faith—to simply hear what God has done for us. Somehow we think our stories alone should build their faith. "God did it for us," we say. "See?" But kingdom discipleship doesn't work that way.

ACTION

1. When was the last time you had a heart-to-heart conversation with another man in an effort to either disciple or be discipled?

2. What can you do to increase the frequency that these types of times with other men take place in your life?

3. What do you think hinders men from getting together in authentic relationships to disciple and be discipled?

PRAYER

Jesus, I want to grow in my ability to share what God has done in my life with other men. I want to develop more authentic relationships with men where I can foster this growth and open doors for learning and discovering all You have for me to accomplish regarding Your kingdom. In Your name, amen.

SIXTY

The things which you have heard from me in the presence of many witnesses, entrust these to faithful men who will be able to teach others also.

2 Timothy 2:2

The cycle of generational transfer is an ongoing process if it is to work at all. A memorial you create, like the "stones of remembrance" we read about in Joshua, or other ways to remember God's work in your life, is never enough on its own. We've all seen what happens to unattended memorials. They get overgrown with weeds. In fact, most of us don't even know why a lot of memorials are there.

Trophy cases often get stuffed to the brim, only to become covered in dust. Life goes on, and we forget to even look. Kingdom men are to never forget what God has done. Kingdom men are to have a transferable faith through engaged communication, not just memorials, trophies, or stones of remembrance stacked high. Our testimony needs to come from our hearts, be fresh on our lips, and impact the lives of those with whom we have contact.

We are facing a massive values-transfer failure in our country and Christian culture because we have neglected to tell those under our care about what God has done in our lives. We have neglected to have the long conversations about not only our spiritual victories but also our spiritual failures. We have neglected to go into the specific details of lessons learned through our sins. While we might have pointed at our miracle moments and said, "Look what God did," that's not enough to disciple someone else. That's not the whole story. We hide the past pains and sins so we don't end up teaching much of anything at all. As a result, we have failed to empower the generations after us to move forward into their own experience of God.

ACTION

1. What keeps you from sharing about your past failures or sins to help others learn?

2. What would you need to happen for you to become bolder in sharing your testimony—not just the positive points but also the negative?

3. Have you ever learned anything important from someone else's lessons in life? If so, what was it?

Jesus, I don't want my pride to keep me from sharing what I have learned. Show me what I need to do to be a testament to Your grace and truth in a more holistic way. Free me from shame so that I can proclaim the excellencies of Your love. In Your name, amen.

SIXTY-ONE

God said to Moses, "I AM WHO I AM"; and He said, "Thus you shall say to the sons of Israel, 'I AM has sent me to you.'"

Exodus 3:14

The name God used when He introduced himself to humanity was very straightforward. It was "I AM WHO I AM." God is not an idol to be stuck somewhere out of sight. God is the God of this moment in time. He is the living, active God who leads and guides us. Each generation must be told about the ever-present nature of God regularly. That's how they are taught to look for Him in the *now* moments of life. Otherwise, God becomes someone distant and formal—like a ritual to take part in.

Those you seek to transfer kingdom values to must be encouraged to walk with God themselves and experience His hand themselves in each moment of life. That's how they, in turn, rise up as kingdom men.

Each of us as kingdom men are to continually look for God in our present realities. We are to teach those who come behind us not to rely on our experiences alone but to learn from them and then walk into their own. We must never be content to hold up our own spiritual breakthroughs as if the existence of them were enough to leave an imprint. The transfer comes through the telling. That's how we pass on the kingdom principles of biblical manhood. We pass them on by continually talking about what God has done while simultaneously encouraging others to experience Him for themselves. Only then will there be something for the next generation to pass on as well.

ACTION

1. What causes you to consider God in everyday moments?

2. What are some hindrances to recognizing God's hand in the routine aspects of life?

3. Why is it important to look for God in your present reality?

PRAYER

Jesus, increase my spiritual sensitivities so I can recognize You more in the everyday. Show me how to engage with You on a greater level, including the routine times when I may overlook Your involvement. In Your name, amen.

> "For the LORD your God dried up the waters of the Jordan before you until you had crossed, just as the LORD your God had done to the Red Sea, which He dried up before us until we had crossed; that all the peoples of the earth may know that the hand of the LORD is mighty, so that you may fear the LORD your God forever."
>
> Joshua 4:23–24

When you read Joshua 4, you'll discover how setting up markers or memorials can help you not only in your own personal faith but also in transferring kingdom values to others. The people in this chapter set up a marker so that "all the peoples of the earth may know that the hand of the LORD is mighty, so that you may fear the LORD your God forever" (Joshua 4:24). The memorial was not only to remind themselves and the next generation, producing a greater fear of God in their hearts, but it was also there to proclaim God's might to the world.

The Israelites were crossing over into the promised land. The problem in the promised land, though, was that it was full of evil. God wanted the Israelites to know that even though evil would surround them, He had them in His hand. God also wanted the Canaanites, Hittites,

Amorites, and others to hear the stories about what He had done for the Israelites. He wanted them to hear of the miracles He had done in their midst. He chose to show off what He had done so their enemies would know His strength. That way they would gain a better idea of what, and whom, they were up against. God set out to establish the reputation of the Israelites as a nation whose God was over all.

It is unfortunate that the generation of men rising up in our Christian culture hear about very few spiritual memorials in the transfer of the faith. We need to turn this around. We need to remember those times when God showed up and showed out, stepping into our situations to do something everyone thought was impossible. We are never to forget those times. We must also be intentional about making these miraculous moments known to others so they will fear God and honor Him too.

ACTION

1. Describe any reminders or markers you have that help you reflect on God's involvement in your life. But if you don't have any, have you witnessed someone else's?

2. Why is it important to consider God's past actions as we approach our present realities?

3. What are some things that cause us to quickly forget what God has done for us in the past and that inhibit us from telling others?

PRAYER

Jesus, I want to remember Your movement in my life on a more regular basis so that I can draw from those seasons a deeper level of faith and courage for what I face right now. Show me how to set up markers to help me remember Your faithful hand in all things. In Your name, amen.

SIXTY-THREE

> Then David took the Philistine's head and brought it to Jerusalem, but he put his weapons in his tent.
>
> 1 Samuel 17:54

Have you ever wished God would do something miraculous in your life? You have read about Him opening the seas or healing the lame or feeding the thousands with just sardines and crackers. But what has He done for you? If you take a moment to think back, you may discover He already has done something for you. But you forgot to establish a reminder in your life. Life gets busy and we often forget the victories of the past as we face new issues in the present.

But Red Seas don't open up every day. Jordan Rivers don't stop flowing every day. Giants don't fall every day. So when they do, we need to ensure that we remember those times. We need to make sure that we tell the story regularly to others, and that we let the unbelieving world witness the power of our great God.

For example, when David killed Goliath, he took the giant's enormous sword and put it in his own tent. He did that for one reason. That sword served as a perpetual reminder that if any other nine-foot-six fool were to come against the people of the living God, he would meet the same end.

Similarly, kingdom men ought to be sharing about the transformation of lives, the marriages that were saved, the dignity that was restored, and the spiritual victories that have taken place. We are to transfer the experiences of God in our midst—small or large—through authentic relationships built on mutual trust so that we never forget the power of the past, which can be accessed in the present through faith in a mighty God.

ACTION

1. How frequently do you share God's work in your life with others?

2. What are some things or thoughts that keep you from sharing it more often than you do?

3. Has anyone ever encouraged you to grow in your faith by sharing about God's engagement in their life and faith? What did you learn or do as a result?

PRAYER

Jesus, give me a greater boldness and a more confident courage to share my faith and my testimonies of what You have done with others. Help me not to shrink back from opportunities to speak of Your power. In fact, help me to pursue these opportunities more proactively. In Your name, amen.

SIXTY-FOUR

> A good man leaves an inheritance to his children's children, and the wealth of the sinner is stored up for the righteous.
>
> Proverbs 13:22

So many of the issues and devolution in our culture can be directly tied to the lack of a kingdom-based values-transfer to the next generation. This is one reason why we have a generation rising up who are in many ways crippled and confused by their anxiety, anger, blame, hypersensitivities, and more.

I'm sure you've seen enough Olympic races where the dreams of the team came crashing to the ground simply due to a slip of the hand. Even though the team may have been out ahead of the others, their race was abruptly halted when the baton dropped. An essential key to winning any relay involves the passing of the baton. It doesn't matter how fast a runner got out of the blocks or how fast he or she ran if they dropped what was in their hand.

Life is no different. You must pass on kingdom values in this race or it's game over for everyone. Being a kingdom man never stops with you. If it does, then you aren't a kingdom man at all. Faith is not a one-person race. A kingdom man leaves a legacy of a spiritual inheritance to others.

ACTION

1. What kingdom-based values have been transferred to you by others, and what did that process look like?
2. How active and intentional are you in passing on kingdom values to those within your sphere of influence?
3. Why do you think God wants us to live intentionally to influence others for His power and His purposes?

PRAYER

Jesus, I need to be more intentional about passing on kingdom values to everyone I have the opportunity to do so with. Show me how to do this in a strategic and effective way. I want to please You and build up Your kingdom so that the world feels the impact of Your love and Your rule. In Your name, amen.

SIXTY-FIVE

> They were continually devoting themselves to the apostles' teaching and to fellowship, to the breaking of bread and to prayer.
>
> Acts 2:42

We live in the day of instant everything. People want instant food. Instant entertainment. Instant shopping. Instant gratification. Instant relationships. Instant you-name-it. But there are many valuable things in this life that simply don't come about instantly. A transfer of kingdom values is one of them. Discipleship isn't a sprint relay. It's a marathon relay. And marathons are taxing. They are tiring. Runners have to build endurance just to race in a marathon and finish, let alone win.

One of the reasons we have so many men walking away from their responsibility to influence their families and the culture for good is that they have not learned to strategize for long-term gain. It could be that they gave too much too soon and burned out. Or they got bored and lost interest. Or maybe they bail when they don't see any immediate return on their investments of time and attention in others. We live in such an instant-gratification culture that personal values like commitment and diligence are quickly waning. You could say values like that are disappearing before our eyes—almost instantly. Yet, whatever the challenges, we need more men willing to step up to, and stay in, the battle for biblical manhood.

ACTION

1. How has the culture of instant gratification negatively impacted the approach to and process of spiritual discipleship?

2. In what ways has it negatively impacted you and your own willingness to be discipled or to disciple others?

3. What is one approach you can take to curb these negative consequences in your life and in the lives of those you love?

PRAYER

Jesus, grant me the grace to slow down and realize that good things come to those who know how to invest what is needed to gain them. Keep me from the love of instant gratification in all areas of my life. Help me to understand the importance of patience mixed with wisdom, especially when it comes to this area of influencing others for Your kingdom. In Your name, amen.

When Jesus then saw His mother, and the disciple whom He loved standing nearby, He said to His mother, "Woman, behold, your son!" Then He said to the disciple, "Behold, your mother!" From that hour the disciple took her into his own household.

John 19:26–27

I'm sure you've seen the word *legacy* attached to sports, athletes, business owners, employees, volunteers, mentors, coaches, friends, and more, because it's all about passing down the DNA of greatness. These principles apply to all of us in the body of Christ too. Thus, the question each of us must address is, What kind of legacy are we leaving? And what does Scripture say about how we are to further the futures of those we influence?

Each of us plays a part in caring for and influencing the next generation. Each of us affects the future. You get to decide if you want to affect it for good by raising up more kingdom men. And keep in mind, no one is too young to do his part. This concept of passing on a legacy doesn't only apply to parents or grandparents or pastors.

Maybe you are not in a situation where you have children to raise. Or perhaps yours are grown. Maybe you never had kids, or you're too young to have kids, or you're not even married. If any of this applies to you, what I want you to keep in mind is that the legacy you leave behind, whether familial or relational, should be based on these shared biblical principles of transferring kingdom values to the next generation. You *are* leaving a legacy with your life, whether you realize it or not. It may not be a good legacy, but you are making a generational impact through what you do—or don't do. Whether those you influence are your biological seed or not makes little difference in the family of God.

ACTION

1. Define *legacy* in your own words.
2. Why is it important to leave a spiritual legacy?
3. What are you doing to invest in your spiritual legacy?

PRAYER

Jesus, I am leaving a legacy with my life. I am influencing those under my care with the principles of Your kingdom. Help me to be more intentional about this so I can make the most of the time You have gifted me with on earth. Help me to measure my moments and my days so that I do not waste them on what is frivolous and temporal. In Your name, amen.

SIXTY-SEVEN

"As for you, be fruitful and multiply; populate the earth abundantly and multiply in it."

Genesis 9:7

At the beginning of time, God told Adam to fill the earth. God didn't give him that instruction just because He was bored and wanted to fill the earth for the sake of filling it. No, Adam was to fill the earth with the image of God. Humanity is made in the image of God. Each of us is to leave our mark on others, to affect people so that the reflection of God and His kingdom values continues to be replicated in history.

The legacy we are to pass down to others through God's inheritance never starts with giving them stuff. I'm not saying there is anything wrong with stuff. Nor am I speaking against prospering financially or prudently planning to leave a financial inheritance through a will. But what I am saying is if you pass on stuff without the spiritual, it will dissolve in the hands of those you give it to like cotton candy in the mouth of the one who consumes it. Cotton candy might taste sweet for a second, but it has absolutely zero long-term value.

Adam wasn't commissioned to fill the earth with accolades, achievements, and material wealth. He was to fill the earth with the image of God. A divine inheritance isn't about houses, clothes, cars, fame, or money. Divine inheritances start with the transfer of the faith. It doesn't matter how much money a person has if he or she does not have the foundation of a solid faith. Without biblical values, it will all come crashing down when the storms of life roll in. Every kingdom man must be about passing on the spiritual inheritance of a comprehensive theistic world view.

ACTION

1. What do you think is God's purpose in creating humanity in His image?
2. What kinds of strategies does Satan employ to remove this image or remove humanity from existence?
3. In what ways can the church resist Satan's strategies so that more kingdom followers can be created to influence the culture for Christ?

Jesus, I want to focus on passing down a spiritual inheritance to those around me and not just stuff, money, or my personal goals for their lives. Help me to have a greater level of discernment so that I can recognize what is truly important when I am seeking to impact others made in Your image. In Your name, amen.

"Now may God give you of the dew of heaven, and of the fatness of the earth, and an abundance of grain and new wine; may peoples serve you, and nations bow down to you; be master of your brothers, and may your mother's sons bow down to you. Cursed be those who curse you, and blessed be those who bless you."

Genesis 27:28–29

Two predominant grids operate on this earth: humanism and theism. Humanism focuses on mankind and what mankind wants, thinks, and determines. Functioning according to humanism is like putting on sunglasses filtered to reveal the ego's world view. Conversely, theism filters everything through the lens of God's eternal perspective and divine truth.

As kingdom men, we are created and called to transfer a theistic viewpoint to those within our spheres of influence. In this way, we pass on the DNA of the covenant infused in the dominion mandate found in Genesis. We are to pass on the blessing (see Genesis 1:28). The blessing is based on the spiritual. This concept of passing on the inheritance, or transferring the blessing, is a very big deal in the Bible, as it should be today. Especially because the blessing involves the future. It's so much more than a saying to offer someone after they sneeze or a pat on the back with some positive words.

The blessing, when carried out according to God's covenantal rule, always includes divine favor. It involves the furthering of a great future for whomever it is given to based on God's inheritance.

ACTION

1. Describe the differences between humanism and theism in your own words.

2. What is the prominent influence on the body of Christ right now?

3. What are some of the resistances the culture has, as well as the Christian culture, to living according to a theistic world view?

PRAYER

Jesus, divine favor from God makes all the difference in the world. I want it for my own life, and I want it for the lives of those I love. Help me to access divine favor through all I do and say. Give me wisdom on how to pass this divine favor down to those I love as well. In Your name, amen.

SIXTY-NINE

"And I will make you a great nation, and I will bless you, and make your name great; and so you shall be a blessing; and I will bless those who bless you, and the one who curses you I will curse. And in you all the families of the earth will be blessed."

Genesis 12:2–3

As a kingdom man, you have the freedom and opportunity to bless those within your spheres of influence. The blessing is a declaration of divine benefit, divine protection, and divine dominion. This is what we've been called to transfer to the next generation as kingdom men operating our lives underneath the comprehensive rule of God. It's not about giving those you bless a goal or a future role to aim toward. Let them choose their own goals and roles based on their own thoughts and desires. Neither is it about giving them stuff, as we've looked at in earlier devotions. Rather, transferring the blessing is always about affirming God's favor and will for the lives of those who are being blessed.

Keep in mind, to be blessed in the Bible meant you were to also become a blessing to others. It's never only about you.

When you seek to pass on the blessing to someone else, or when you seek to receive a blessing from someone else, remember that it is not about helping someone make a name for themselves. Or you, for that matter. It isn't even about identifying skills and talents to explore. Living in the kingdom blessing means learning to live in divine favor, which then spills out onto how others both perceive and treat you. It is about what God wants to do in you, for you, and through you.

ACTION

1. Of the three aspects of a blessing—divine benefit, divine protection and divine dominion—which is most important to you and why?

2. Why is it important to allow those you seek to bless the freedom to make their own decisions about their future?

3. Have you ever been held back by someone trying to dictate your choices under the guise of blessing? What was the result?

Jesus, make me an instrument of Your divine benefit, divine protection, and divine dominion to those around me. I want to be a conduit of the blessing from God to others. Show me what I need to adjust in my own life to position myself to live this out more fully. In Your name, amen.

SEVENTY

> Listen, O my people, to my instruction; incline your ears to the words of my mouth. I will open my mouth in a parable; I will utter dark sayings of old, which we have heard and known, and our fathers have told us. We will not conceal them from their children, but tell to the generation to come the praises of the LORD, and His strength and His wondrous works that He has done.
>
> Psalm 78:1–4

Passing on the blessing isn't just about the pass itself. It's also about clearing the field of any known blockers in the way. You can do this by acknowledging where you dropped the ball and cost one for the team. It's owning your mistakes and letting others know you are sorry that your mistakes or failures negatively affected them. That goes a long way in removing the baggage that could block the transfer of the blessing. If you know of an area where you've let someone down, even if it was in the past, it is still a healing thing to take the time now to let them know you are sorry.

Transferring the principles of biblical manhood should ultimately lead to future spiritual leadership, especially if you are willing to admit that you blew it. When you are authentic about the transfer and seek to do it well, the next generation will be positioned to witness their own Jericho walls fall down. They'll get their own victories over Ai. They'll cross their own Jordan Rivers. They will topple their own giants with a stone and a slingshot. They will do so because you have given them the tools they need to live out God's kingdom plan for their lives.

In turn, the next generation will then lead others and raise up future kingdom men who do not follow the crowd. They will do this because they will grab the mantle of the blessing, favor, and authority of God.

ACTION

1. What did you learn from a personal experience of confessing a past mistake and apologizing for it?
2. How can it be helpful to share how you dropped the ball in past decisions?
3. How have you benefited from other people's authenticity in sharing about their own mistakes or sins?

PRAYER

Jesus, being completely honest and admitting where I have fallen short is something that I ask You to help me do more willingly and freely than I ever have before. Let me be an example of authentic communication as I seek to disciple those under my personal influence and care. In Your name, amen.

For the LORD is good; His lovingkindness is everlasting and His faithfulness to all generations.

Psalm 100:5

You may not have had the blessing handed down to you by a father, grandfather, uncle, coach, pastor, leader, or friend. You may feel alone and lost, unable to become all you know you were created to be. But if you choose to honor God through your heart and actions, the transference of kingdom covenantal blessings is yours for the asking. It's never too late to secure your legacy from God.

Things might look funny to you right now. Maybe you've been scrambling around trying to figure life out. Or maybe you've been knocked down so many times you can no longer get back up on your own, and you need a hand to seize. Whatever the case, God can set things straight again. He can bring people into your life to help you when you need it. He can put you back on your feet again.

God wants you to have the blessing as much as you want to have it. What you've got to do is look to Him, honor Him with your heart and actions, and then ask Him to release the full favor of His blessing and authority on you. Once that's done, you are positioned to transfer the values of the kingdom of God to those within your circle of influence. Each of us can leave a legacy of greatness wherever we are as we rise up as kingdom men.

ACTION

1. What parts of the blessing have you experienced being handed down to you, if any?
2. What parts of the blessing do you wish you had received more fully from those who went before you?
3. In what areas can you express to God that you desire to have a greater manifestation of His blessing?

PRAYER

Jesus, I ask for the blessing and favor of God in my life. Though there may be things I did not receive from those who were over my care and discipleship, I ask that You would intervene on my behalf to ensure that I am positioned to receive all of the blessing that God has reserved for me. In Your name, amen.

SEVENTY-TWO

> Whatever you do, do your work heartily, as for the Lord
> rather than for men, knowing that from the Lord you will
> receive the reward of the inheritance. It is the Lord Christ
> whom you serve.
>
> Colossians 3:23–24

You can measure the destiny of a team—whether that be a family, work group, business, church, community, or even nation—by its leadership. Unfortunately, today we face a crisis of leadership. People don't know who to follow anymore because this crisis has produced a plethora of poor models and mentors and a complete and utter lack of great leaders.

Yet, God's kingdom program is designed around this process of transferring spiritual wisdom, known as discipleship, in order to produce future leaders. One of the primary roles of kingdom men is to lead others in the way they should go. Another term we often use for leaders is *influencers*. The issue is never whether a man is a leader. As a kingdom man, you are one by nature of your calling. The issue is whether you will be a great leader or a poor one.

To be a poor leader requires little effort on your part. But to be a leader who truly influences those around you to rise up and pursue the advancement of God's kingdom agenda requires a level of courage unlike what many have today. It is countercultural to lead people in biblical values. Only men who understand and embrace this reality will be able to suffer the slings of the enemy with dignity and grace as they pursue the preparation of the next generation to serve Christ.

ACTION

1. How does a crisis of leadership show up in a church setting?
2. How does a crisis of leadership show up in a family setting?
3. How does a crisis of leadership show up in a cultural setting?

PRAYER

Jesus, make me part of the solution and not part of the problem. I do not want to contribute to a crisis of leadership in any form or manner. Raise my own internal standards of what it means to truly live as a kingdom man so that I fully live out and experience the leadership role I am called to fulfill. In Your name, amen.

SEVENTY-THREE

> So you will again distinguish between the righteous and the wicked, between one who serves God and one who does not serve Him.
>
> Malachi 3:18

Raising up a generation of key influencers is never to be done in a top-down way. It happens organically and authentically when men share their lives, experiences, and conversations. Developing key influencers who can solidly speak on biblical truths and navigate the storms of society requires guidance, practice, learning, listening, and so forth. Just like any marriage is dependent on two people contributing for it to be great, identifying and raising up a kingdom influencer requires both men to put forth the effort to learn, grow, listen, teach, discern, practice, model, and more.

One of the most important aspects of someone becoming a kingdom disciple is their willingness and desire to become a kingdom disciple. You cannot disciple someone who is not interested in growing and developing themselves. Make sure you keep your eyes open for those whom God places in your path who are open to learning about God and maturing spiritually. Otherwise, you may be wasting your time. A healthy tree produces healthy fruit. You can know someone's intentions and heart by looking at the fruit they produce around them.

As we come together to mentor and to model for each other what true biblical manhood looks like, we are rising up collectively as kingdom men to impact our homes, churches, communities, nation, and world for God and for good.

ACTION

1. Why is it important to not approach discipleship of future influencers in a top-down way?

2. Have you ever tried to disciple or mentor someone who just wasn't interested, and if so, what did you learn from that process?

3. What are ways the body of Christ can encourage men to have a greater desire to grow and develop spiritually?

PRAYER

Jesus, let me be sensitive enough to discern who desires to grow spiritually and who doesn't. Help me to invest my time and energy into those who want to develop as kingdom men. Show me ways I can do that even more than I am today. In Your name, amen.

SEVENTY-FOUR

Beloved, do not believe every spirit, but test the spirits to see whether they are from God, because many false prophets have gone out into the world.

1 John 4:1

Identifying God's hand on a man will have a direct impact on the legacy you leave behind. Who you choose to invest in will reflect back on you. Just like a football coaching tree either reflects poorly or greatly on its members, who you disciple and what they choose to do with their lives after being impacted by you will reflect upon you.

Multiple attributes can help you either identify a potential influencer or set yourself up to be identified by others. Every man holds within himself the potential to rise up as a key influencer in his circle. What we need now, more than ever, is a group of kingdom men rising up to tackle the challenges our churches and culture face. Character qualities and relationship norms such as mutual commitment, a servant spirit, and a great faith will help bring this about.

A kingdom influencer knows how to remain committed through the tough times as well as through the good.

Commitment requires sacrifice, setting your own wants and desires aside, and living with a long-term view of life's meaning and purposes.

ACTION

1. Name two or three individuals you feel God may be leading you to invest in through discipleship and mentoring.

2. What steps do you need to take to move toward discipling these individuals more seriously?

3. Consider someone who may be able and willing to disciple you, and after prayer, approach them to see if they will.

PRAYER

Jesus, I ask for greater courage and clarity when it comes to influencing those in my care. Show me what I need to do to step up to the plate and live as the man of God You have created me to be. If there is someone who can disciple me to grow and develop more fully as well, show me who that is and place a willingness in his heart to do so. In Your name, amen.

SEVENTY-FIVE

This is My commandment, that you love one another, just as I have loved you. Greater love has no one than this, that one lay down his life for his friends. You are My friends if you do what I command you.

John 15:12–14

To exercise your biblical manhood through a position of influence, you need to know where you are headed. You need to have a vision. Visions aren't often birthed in silos. Visions are formulated through studying the lessons of the past and the leaders of the present and combining that with your calling and the calling of those under your care.

A man can do this by listening to those above him and around him. A great mind remains moldable and open to learning from others and following guidance with humility. A great leader constantly works on improving his skills and his game. One way to do this is by studying, listening, and asking questions of those in leadership roles. Kingdom leadership requires both following and leading through a mutual commitment expressed in both men in a relationship, or in the groups of men being poured into.

To live apart from relationships that allow you to encourage and edify each other is to live apart from the mandate to make disciples and also to grow spiritually yourself. Life on life is where growth takes place. This requires intentionality, humility, and most important—commitment.

ACTION

1. Where do you see yourself in five years from a spiritual and influential standpoint?
2. What steps do you need to take this week and this year to set yourself on the path to achieve the five-year vision you have for yourself?
3. In what ways can you listen more openly to godly men who have been placed in your life to influence you for good?

PRAYER

Jesus, I hope that, through listening and learning to the wisdom of those who have grown more than I have, I will continue to develop into a kingdom man who can impact and influence others. I want to develop more personal relationships with men that will allow us all to benefit and develop more fully. In Your name, amen.

SEVENTY-SIX

> Let us not lose heart in doing good, for in due time we will reap if we do not grow weary.
>
> Galatians 6:9

Achieving greatness in this life often comes as a result of merging mutual strengths together. Rarely does one man rise to accomplish tremendous things all on his own. There's typically a coach, parent, mentor, pastor, friend, neighbor, teammate, sibling, or teacher—or a combination of those and more—who helps create the context for success. Kingdom men recognize the value of and need for contributors in every aspect of the equation who are committed to a shared overarching goal.

Unfortunately, commitment has gone missing. We don't see a lot of commitment around. People quit very easily in our culture, especially when things get tough. Half of all marriages end in divorce. Couples simply give up and quit on each other. Career hopping has become the new normal, with employees quitting after just a year or two to go do something new. It is often linked to the increased pressure that comes with increased responsibilities as jobs develop over time. Just as an employee enters that second or third year when roles get fine-tuned and bigger tasks start to get assigned, tenacity gets lost. So they start over somewhere else.

A kingdom leader transfers this value of commitment by demonstrating it and then by identifying and choosing those who value commitment as well.

ACTION

1. Describe what happens when you stop seeing results from the investment of your time and energy in a project or person?

2. How does Galatians 6:9 speak into this situation?

3. How has our contemporary culture impacted individuals' ability to persevere with tenacity and diligence?

PRAYER

Jesus, enable me to keep going even when I don't see any fruit for the effort I am putting forward. Remind me how important it is to keep the faith and trust the outcome to Your hands. Please also give me hints along the way to help me know that I am not alone in my desire to impact other people's lives. In Your name, amen.

"But the greatest among you shall be your servant."

Matthew 23:11

A fundamental rule of biblical manhood is that you don't get to the top without serving first. You don't wake up number one. What's more, a true kingdom man never stops serving.

Unfortunately, today we have a lot of men who want to skip serving and get to the top quick. They want to skip the hard work, dedication, and tenacity required for greatness. I have had young pastors ask me numerous times over the years what the secret is for building a church the size and scope of ours. I know what they mean by the question because there really is no secret at all. They are looking for a secret, but none exists. Common sense tells you it took hard work, grit, commitment, and humility through serving when no one was watching, the lights were out, and no one knew your name. Effort has become a lost quality in our land.

It takes hard work to unleash and achieve greatness, no matter what industry you are in. And a good part of that hard work involves your willingness to serve. Jesus put it this way, "But the greatest among you shall be your servant."

1. What are some thoughts you entertain that keep you from proactively seeking to serve others or becoming more involved in your local body of believers?

2. What would happen to an athletic team that lost their willingness to put in the effort to stay physically fit during the off-season?

3. In what ways has the culture reshaped humanity's thinking to have increased desire for quick success and instant fame?

PRAYER

Jesus, I am willing to be patient as You move me along the pathway of development and growth. I am willing to serve those around me. I understand that life isn't about me and my desires. It is about connecting with others who share similar values and goals so that together we can advance Your kingdom agenda on earth. In Your name, amen.

SEVENTY-EIGHT

> But He answered them, "My Father is working until now, and I Myself am working."
>
> John 5:17

We have far too many men who want to lead but don't want to follow. They want to lead but refuse to serve. They want to skip straight to number one without any experience at being number two, three, or even ten. But great leaders, great coaches, great men know that you only transfer authority and responsibility to those who have demonstrated the ability to handle it.

You ascend to greatness by descending into a role of service first. No one has ever woken up as the president of a company or a chairman of the board. Key leaders serve their way to the top by performing in a manner that demonstrates the willingness, understanding, character, and responsibility to pull off even greater things.

That is a truism of life itself. Joshua had the privilege of the mountaintop experience because he was willing to serve in the valley. What's more, he was wise enough to serve. Kingdom men realize that to get somewhere in life, you need to learn from those who have gotten somewhere in life. You need to listen. Take notes. Observe. Ask questions. Contribute. Study. Respect. Acknowledge. And serve.

ACTION

1. What are some practical ways you can start serving more?

2. Have you observed anyone ascend the ladder of notoriety who carried with him or her a servant's heart? What did you learn from observing them?

3. How does our culture portray those who are willing to serve others, and does this positively or negatively impact people's desire to serve?

PRAYER

Jesus, correct my thinking where I am wrong about the value of serving and investing in others. Give me biblical insight so I can see and understand how You view a servant's heart. Help me live for an audience of One, knowing that Your approval and favor is more meaningful than anything else I could ever have in my life. In Your name, amen.

SEVENTY-NINE

> "Be strong and courageous, do not be afraid or tremble at them, for the LORD your God is the one who goes with you. He will not fail you or forsake you."
>
> Deuteronomy 31:6

A lot of men are not growing spiritually because they are not positioning themselves for growth. They are not placing themselves in the proximity of spiritual greatness. You can't run with carnal Christians and expect to rise as a kingdom man. You have to look for men who are already in the right spot. They may not be perfect, but they are close to God. In fact, that's one reason the disciples became such dynamic men. They knew where to hang out. They spent time with Christ. They knew to reject the spirit of fear in all things.

Any man who only sees how big the problem is does not have the spiritual DNA of a kingdom man. I sure don't need men around me telling me how big a problem is. Do you? If there's a giant, he's giant! You don't need to tell me he is a giant. But kingdom men remember who they are. They remember they are giant-slayers. They are Baal fighters, like Gideon. Kingdom men don't run when they face a giant. Instead, they figure out how to maneuver around, climb over, barrel through, or simply out-strategize the opponent. Bottom line: Kingdom men don't cower when giants tower over them.

Whatever you are facing today, even if it is looming large, casting shadows of doubt and producing feelings of fear, remember who you are in Christ. Remember the tools He has given you called faith, courage, and the rightful use of His name. You can overcome anything when you are connected to the One who rules over all. Let your hope rest in this truth.

ACTION

1. Describe what you are doing to position yourself for growth spiritually and also from an influencer standpoint.

2. In what ways can you make yourself even more available to face and overcome obstacles?

3. What are some thoughts you have that encourage you to run or turn from conflict, especially spiritually based conflict, when the need is there for you to rise up and confront it?

Jesus, increase my courage. Pour into me a greater level of faith that strengthens me when life's situations turn sour. Help me to stand up and act like a man of God in order to overcome whatever I'm facing. I ask for Your Spirit to be made manifest within me at a greater level than ever before. In Your name, amen.

I can do all things through Him who strengthens me.

Philippians 4:13

Scripture has already made it clear that we can do all things through Christ who strengthens us. That's the criterion you are to base your decisions on. Is God leading you into battle? Is God asking you to speak up at work? Has God placed a problem in your path that He wants you to influence and sort out for others' good and His glory? If God has given the challenge to you or allowed it into your life, then you are man enough to face it head on and overcome.

I understand that you may have had a difficult upbringing. I am not denying that there are inequities and disparities still at play in our culture. I'm fully aware that broken systems contribute to broken structures, which can lead to broken lives. But it's not about the giant standing in front of you. It's about what you hold in your hand. What experience, awareness, skill, or tool has God given you to overcome the opposition?

Whatever it is, use it. I've been around long enough to know that despite all the talk and well-wishes and protests, systems rarely change completely. Embedded structures are often difficult to improve holistically, and prejudices often remain—whether it is prejudice against a particular race, culture, class, or background. It doesn't matter the details; what matters is what's in your hand and how you are going to rise above that which seeks to hold you hostage or keep you down.

ACTION

1. At what level and in what ways do you apply Philippians 4:13 to your life?

2. How have any difficulties or setbacks or even unfair treatment of you in your past negatively affected decisions you have made?

3. What can you do to better let go of the past and focus with a pure and faith-filled heart on your present situations?

PRAYER

Jesus, I ask for Your help in letting go of any bitterness or regret that I still carry from things that have happened to me in my past. Show me what I must do to live with a pure, trusting heart in my present moments so that I do not drag past pain into my decisions. I ask that You would enable me to look to my future with a heart full of hope, knowing that You have a good plan up ahead for me if I will remain faithful to You through all things. In Your name, amen.

EIGHTY-ONE

"I call heaven and earth to witness against you today, that I have set before you life and death, the blessing and the curse. So choose life in order that you may live, you and your descendants, by loving the Lord your God, by obeying His voice, and by holding fast to Him; for this is your life and the length of your days, that you may live in the land which the Lord swore to your fathers, to Abraham, Isaac, and Jacob, to give them."

Deuteronomy 30:19–20

Adversity and challenges have a way, if you let them, of sharpening your skills, strengthening your will, and focusing your approach to your goals and dreams. They can cause you to rise higher than people ever expected you to go, or higher than you thought you would go. But it all depends on how you choose to view and respond to the difficulties that come your way. Will you respond in great faith, or will you respond in blame, bitterness, or fear? It's your choice. But whatever choice you make will also determine the outcome you, and generations after you, face.

We are living in a day when the proverbial fork in the road is more pronounced than ever. When you examine all that is happening around us—the chaos, confusion, lack of clarity, and voices coming at us from all directions—it is clear that it is time for men to make a choice. Will you choose wisely and live? Or will you choose poorly? Cultural change starts with one man making one wise decision and then the next. And it starts right now.

ACTION

1. Describe a time you "chose death" through your actions. What was the result?

2. How often are we to "choose life" through our words, thoughts, and actions?

3. What would it take to see a true cultural impact of kingdom values in our land today?

PRAYER

Jesus, focus my thoughts and my goals on everyday life so that I do not miss opportunities to choose life in all I think, say, and do. Encourage me through Your presence so that I can see the impact wisdom has not only on my life but on the lives of those around me. In Your name, amen.

EIGHTY-TWO

Be on the alert, stand firm in the faith, act like men, be strong.

1 Corinthians 16:13

Kingdom men live a life that both models and guides others on how to live according to spiritual principles of manhood. When David went up against Goliath, he faced awful odds according to the world's standards. Everyone was calling on Goliath to win, and to win easily. Many men would have cowered beneath an opponent the world predicted to win. But that's not what kingdom men do. Kingdom men don't cower. Kingdom men don't listen to the odds. Kingdom men rise to overcome the obstacles at hand. They certainly don't run from them.

As kingdom men, we are to rise above the obstacles looming large before us in our land. We must never back down or seek to avoid them. Instead, we are to set a new standard. Establish a new pace. Boldly declare that we, as men, no longer accept the evil nor the divisions that the culture demands remain. We must do this for ourselves, but we also must do this with, and for, each other. When you commit to living as a kingdom man, it isn't about being a lone-ranger Christian. You are choosing to identify with men who will collectively respond to the need for a fresh troop of kingdom warriors to take our stand.

ACTION

1. In what ways are you intentionally modeling how to live according to spiritual principles of manhood?

2. In what ways could you use social media to intentionally model how to live according to spiritual principles of manhood more than you already do?

3. Is there anything you need to improve in your life regarding your connection to other godly men or your willingness to disciple others?

PRAYER

Jesus, help me to see how I can be more intentional about modeling what it looks like to live as a fully dedicated kingdom man. Show me where I need to be more willing to connect with other men to be discipled or to disciple others. In Your name, amen.

But the wisdom from above is first pure, then peace-
able, gentle, reasonable, full of mercy and good fruits,
unwavering, without hypocrisy.

James 3:17

As a kingdom man, you understand that your choices
affect not only you but all of those under your care. What
you choose matters. Your decisions impact others. You
can choose life by basing your decisions on the wisdom
of God's Word. His commandments, precepts, and principles exist to show you how to live a life of wisdom.

As you make your choices throughout your days,
there are a lot of conflicting and tempting options out
there. They may seem right. They may look enticing.
But the real question is whether your choice is one that
Jesus himself would authorize and endorse. Because if
it's not what Jesus would authorize or endorse, all you
will experience is disintegration and ultimate death in
whatever it is you are pursuing. Wrong choices lead to
failure, frustration, and loss.

Yet if you choose wisely, the truth of God's Word will
bring life, not only to you but also to those around you.
By applying God's wisdom to your life and by living in

accordance with what He has outlined in Scripture, you are setting yourself up for spiritual success. Wisdom is the way to experience God's will and His favor, because wisdom is the application of God's will to the practical areas of life.

ACTION

1. Describe a time when one of your choices, or a culmination of choices, negatively impacted someone else you love. What did you learn from that?

2. Describe a time when one of your choices, or a culmination of choices, positively impacted someone else you love. What did you learn from that?

3. How can you better seek to know and apply God's truth in your life?

PRAYER

Jesus, my choices impact others for good or for bad. I am not a lone-ranger Christian. What I do has an impact on those I love. Help me to recognize this and take it to heart so that I will walk with wisdom and move forward with grace in all I think, say, and do. In Your name, amen.

EIGHTY-FOUR

The LORD arises to contend, and stands to judge the
people. The LORD enters into judgment with the elders
and princes of His people, "It is you who have devoured
the vineyard; the plunder of the poor is in your houses."

Isaiah 3:13–14

The choice to live as a kingdom man or not is yours. But
while the choice is yours, I want to remind you that you
don't get to choose the consequences. All consequences
are in the hand of God. Isaiah 3 makes it clear what
happens when men do not choose well. The younger
generation winds up in rebellion, oppression ensues, and
chaos reigns.

As a result of abdicating their biblical kingdom roles,
the men became weak and fell by the sword (Isaiah 3:25).
Unfortunately, this all sounds very familiar. Too many
men are operating outside of their divinely ordained responsibilities, thus causing all of us to fall by the sword of
societal unrest. What we need are men who are willing
not only to declare, as Joshua did in Joshua 24, that they
are kingdom men, but also to live like they are.

This declaration is to be made manifest in what you
think, say, and do. It is to show up in how you carry

yourself in the culture, how you conduct your business dealings, and how you interact with others in the body of Christ. A kingdom man's choices should have a ripple effect on all he comes near to bring about the greater good for everyone and usher in a larger display of God's glory.

ACTION

1. What would you say is God's purpose for applying consequences to our choices?

2. In what way can negative consequences turn into a positive experience in a man's life?

3. Describe a major lesson you learned from experiencing negative consequences.

PRAYER

Jesus, help me never to waste the consequences You allow in my life, which are there to teach me and help me develop into a kingdom man. Give me wisdom to learn and humility to apply what I have learned so that I can grow as a man in order to serve You and Your purposes for my life even more than I ever have before. In Your name, amen.

EIGHTY-FIVE

"If it is disagreeable in your sight to serve the LORD, choose for yourselves today whom you will serve: whether the gods which your fathers served which were beyond the River, or the gods of the Amorites in whose land you are living; but as for me and my house, we will serve the LORD."

Joshua 24:15

One thing that a kingdom man should never forget is that God has an exclusivity clause. He cannot be second. My great concern with all of the cultural turmoil we are going through is that while many men may be calling on God and praying to God, they also have idols competing for and consuming their attention. These so-called American idols are sophisticated. Subtle. An idol might be technology. It could be politics. Celebrities. Sports. Status. It might even be one's race, income, entertainment, or career. As I've stated before, anything that overrules God in your decision-making—including another relationship—is an idol.

When you exalt an idol over God, you have removed Him from the equation. This is because God will excuse himself from participating or intervening, even though you may be praying to Him for help.

It is only when men stand up, stand strong, and declare what is right and true that the influence of positive impact will be felt. Joshua's kingdom declaration in Joshua 24 did not deny the reality of the day nor the humanity of each man, but it did state that these things were to be subject to a higher authority and greater good. To sum it up, he declared that he would put God first.

ACTION

1. What are some idols that take your attention away from God?
2. How have these idols brought you benefit over the course of your life or in any of your relationships?
3. Why is it important to turn from idols and turn toward the living God in all you think, say, and do?

PRAYER

Jesus, reveal to me the areas where I still need to address any hidden idolatry I have in my life. Help me to turn from idolatry and turn toward You in my thoughts and actions. Enable me to disciple other men to recognize idols in their own lives as well. In Your name, amen.

EIGHTY-SIX

Therefore be careful how you walk, not as unwise men but as wise, making the most of your time, because the days are evil. So then do not be foolish, but understand what the will of the Lord is.

Ephesians 5:15–17

Far too many men want a cafeteria god. This is the kind of god that you pick and choose when you want him and when you don't. That's not the kind of God that God is, and that's not the kind of man He is looking to partner with in impacting the world. God doesn't want you just aligning with Him in private. He is not seeking a silent majority. God calls each of us to publicly declare our allegiance to Him above all else. It is then that He will join us to address the issues at hand.

God has something to say on every subject and issue that confronts us as a culture and in our own personal lives, and He has not stuttered. If we are going to make a difference of healing, oneness, justice, and righteousness in a broken world, we must get our own lives together first and then come together in a like-minded approach to impacting the culture. Yes, the past may house its mistakes. But we can start right now to make a better tomorrow. We can start when each man personally declares he will serve God in all he thinks, says, and does. That is not to say you will do this perfectly, but if your intention is to try to make God the priority, He will honor your heart. Once enough of us stand up to live in this conviction, we will begin to see the ripple effect of positive change flood over our land.

ACTION

1. Why is it important to let go of your past and not allow the negativity in it to influence your present and future?

2. In what ways do you proactively place God in the highest position in your life?

3. Have you seen a ripple effect of your actions that had a positive impact on others? What did you learn from it?

PRAYER

Jesus, give me the grace I need to let go of the past and focus on the now. Help me to recognize Your presence in all situations so that I can honor You with my actions. Show me the way to go and the path I need to take in order to live out the destiny You have created me for. In Your name, amen.

EIGHTY-SEVEN

"Declaring the end from the beginning, and from ancient times things which have not been done, saying, 'My purpose will be established, and I will accomplish all My good pleasure.'"

Isaiah 46:10

We face a culture that wants to trick us, trip us up, and get us to make the wrong decisions or give the wrong replies. But the answer to whether we will experience life or death in our walk as men is actually in our own hands. Satan only appears to be winning this war on the world because kingdom men have illegitimately handed him the ball. It's not because Satan is more powerful. He's not. Our futures, and the futures of our families, churches, communities, and nation, are in our own hands. They are based on what we decide.

If we, as kingdom men, collectively choose to follow Christ by cultivating a relationship with Him and submitting to His rule, we will produce life. Any other path we pursue will result in further destruction. The choice is ours to make. The time to make that choice is now.

It is high time we rise up as one voice and one example for each other, our families, our churches, our communities, and our land. It's time we take our positions on the field called life. Grab what you've got. Use it. Make your moves. Sure, your opponents may be tall, strong, or even programmed to beat you. But you know the one who knows the end from the beginning. The one who crafted and created you has already determined His purposes will be carried out.

God will do it. The victory is already His. It's your role to walk in His established purpose for your life. It's your responsibility to intentionally and strategically progress forward.

ACTION

1. What are some ways that Satan seeks to trick us or trip us up as kingdom men?
2. What tools do you have in place to help you so that you do not fall for Satan's tactics?
3. What additional tools could you put in place to make you even more equipped to resist Satan's tactics?

PRAYER

Jesus, I want to overcome any tactic the enemy throws at me, and I need Your wisdom, strength, and presence in my life at a greater level in order to do so. Show me how to find my power in You even more each day. In Your name, amen.

DAY

EIGHTY-EIGHT

> Then David said to his son Solomon, "Be strong and courageous, and act; do not fear nor be dismayed, for the Lord God, my God, is with you. He will not fail you nor forsake you until all the work for the service of the house of the Lord is finished."
>
> 1 Chronicles 28:20

David was a kingdom man who didn't cower in front of a giant. That's one reason God chose him to eventually become king. Saul and the armies of Israel looked on Goliath and trembled. David saw the giant and strategized a plan for his defeat. David didn't let his fear overtake him. In fact, David put his fear in its rightful place.

Likewise, kingdom men are not to run away in the face of adversity. Kingdom men are not to bail out when the going gets tough. You know as well as I do that it is chumps who run in the face of challenge. It is chumps who bail. But true, authentic, and strong kingdom men rise up, because when everyone else is chanting, "We can't," there's one voice that quietly, yet firmly, responds, "Why not?" With God, you can do anything.

If a shepherd boy can slay a giant with a stone, there is no telling what God can do through you and through me. God has given you the tools you need to overcome whatever obstacles you face and to march forward on a mission to expand His glory and advance His kingdom agenda.

ACTION

1. What is your natural inclination when you face conflict or a difficult challenge that could cost you something?

2. What are some reminders you can position in your life to help you regain confidence and faith in God when difficulties come?

3. Where do you think David drew his courage from, especially since he was so young, and what can you learn from him?

PRAYER

Jesus, increase my level of faith and my confidence in You so that I can live more courageously as a kingdom man. I do not want to shrink back when adversity comes my way. I want to be the strong leader my loved ones need me to be for them. In Your name, amen.

EIGHTY-NINE

When I am afraid, I will put my trust in You. In God, whose word I praise, in God I have put my trust; I shall not be afraid. What can mere man do to me?

Psalm 56:3-4

Greatness esteems greatness, which leads to even more greatness and influence. One of the most important traits of an influencer is the ability to identify talents in those he influences and draw them out to their highest level. A kingdom man looks for ways he can help those under his care grow and develop their own spiritual tools and skills. He uses the opportunities God gives him to invest in the lives of others. This then impacts the collective body of Christ as more and more men seek to invest in the spiritual development and growth of others.

God has called you to participate in life in such a way that everyone around you rises higher than they would have without you in their life. There should be a lasting impact that indicates you have been part of someone else's life. This impact can then spread and have a cascading effect on many more people whom you will only find out about in eternity. Think of the day when you will get to meet all of the people you influenced for God and for good through the ripple effect of your influence as a kingdom man. God wants you to make the most of your time to help make the most of the lives of your brothers in Christ.

ACTION

1. How could you seek to impact more people in your life than you already do?

2. What practical steps can you take to expand your reach and identify more people you can influence for God and for good?

3. What personal development do you need to undertake to better equip you for influencing others?

PRAYER

Jesus, will You help me expand my reach into other people's lives so that I can have a greater impact for Your kingdom? Open my heart to a deeper level of compassion and empathy, enabling me to become more intentional about how I spend my time and effort. In Your name, amen.

Now Jabez called on the God of Israel, saying, "Oh that You would bless me indeed and enlarge my border, and that Your hand might be with me, and that You would keep me from harm that it may not pain me!" And God granted him what he requested.

1 Chronicles 4:10

It's hard to transfer something that was never given to you in the first place. Many men never received the blessing from another kingdom man. You may never have had a man guide you toward kingdom values in your personal development. But even if your life has been filled with challenges, difficulties, and spiritual gaps, you can still gain access to the blessing. Divine favor, dominion, and authority are rightfully yours as a child of the King. All you need to do is ask Him for it.

Perhaps you have no lineage worth revisiting. You have no heritage passed down that is worth honoring. Maybe your mom or your dad resented you as it seems that Jabez's mom resented carrying him, naming him "pain." Maybe when you hear other people speaking about families, your heart doesn't fill up with fond memories, but only with an ache.

But Jabez didn't let his name define him. Your past doesn't define you either. Jabez didn't let what other people felt about him or said about him become his identity. Like any kingdom man, Jabez desired more. He desired the blessing. So he went directly to the Source. What's more, he got it. And you can too. Go to God. God has a great blessing in store for you.

ACTION

1. In what ways did you receive a transfer of the biblical blessing, and in what ways do you feel you did not receive it?

2. How can you be sure you are spending your life to pass on the blessing to those under your care?

3. In what ways have others let you know that you have passed the blessing down to them, and how did that make you feel?

PRAYER

Jesus, make me aware of every situation where I can pass the blessing on to someone under my care. Please bring about situations that will give me greater courage and motivation to provide others with a spiritual blessing. Help me lead through loving You and to learn from those who also love You. In Your name, amen.

THE URBAN ALTERNATIVE

The *Urban Alternative (TUA)* equips, empowers and unites Christians to impact *individuals*, *families*, *churches*, and *communities* through a thoroughly kingdom agenda world view. In teaching truth, we seek to transform lives.

The core cause of the problems we face in our personal lives, homes, churches, and societies is a spiritual one; therefore, the only way to address it is spiritually. We've tried political, social, economic, and even religious agendas.

It's time for a **kingdom agenda**.

> *The kingdom agenda can be defined as the visible manifestation of the comprehensive rule of God over every area of life.*

The unifying central theme throughout the Bible is the glory of God and the advancement of His kingdom. The conjoining thread from Genesis to Revelation—from beginning to end—is focused on one thing: God's glory through advancing God's kingdom.

When you do not recognize that theme, the Bible becomes disconnected stories that are great for inspiration but seem to be unrelated in purpose and direction. Understanding the role of the kingdom in Scripture increases the relevancy of this several-thousand-year-old text to your day-to-day living, because the kingdom is not only then; it is now.

The absence of the kingdom's influence in our personal lives, family lives, churches, and communities has led to a deterioration in our world of immense proportions:

- People live segmented, compartmentalized lives because they lack God's kingdom world view.

- Families disintegrate because they exist for their own satisfaction rather than for the kingdom.

- Churches are limited in the scope of their impact because they fail to comprehend that the goal of the church is not the church itself, but the kingdom.

- Communities have nowhere to turn to find real solutions for real people who have real problems because the church has become divided, ingrown, and unable to transform the cultural and political landscape in any relevant way.

The kingdom agenda offers us a way to see and live life with a solid hope by optimizing the solutions of heaven. When God is no longer the final and authoritative standard under which all else falls, order and hope leave with Him. But the reverse of that is true as well: As long as you have God, you have hope. If God is still in the picture, and as long as His agenda is still on the table, it's not over.

Even if relationships collapse, God will sustain you. Even if finances dwindle, God will keep you. Even if dreams die, God will revive you. As long as God and His rule are still the overarching standard in your life, family, church, and community, there is always hope.

Our world needs the King's agenda. Our churches need the King's agenda. Our families need the King's agenda.

We've put together a three-part plan to direct us in healing the divisions and striving for unity as we move toward the goal of truly being one nation under God. This three-part plan calls us to assemble with others in unity, address the issues that divide us, and to act together for social impact. Following this plan, we will see individuals, families, churches, and communities transformed as we follow God's kingdom agenda in every area of our lives. You can request this plan by emailing info@tonyevans.org, or you can find it online at tonyevans.org.

In many major cities, there is a loop that drivers can take when they want to get somewhere on the other side of the city but don't necessarily want to head straight through downtown. This loop will take you close enough to the city so that you can see its towering buildings and skyline, but not close enough to actually experience it.

This is precisely what we, as a culture, have done with God. We have put Him on the "loop" of our personal, family, church, and community lives. He's close enough to be at hand should we need Him in an emergency, but far enough away that He can't be the center of who we are.

We want God on the loop, not the King of the Bible who comes downtown into the very heart of our ways. Leaving God on the loop brings about dire consequences, as we have seen in our own lives and with others. But when we make God, and His rule, the centerpiece of all we think, do, and say, it is then that we will experience Him in the way He longs for us to experience Him.

He wants us to be kingdom people with kingdom minds set on fulfilling His kingdom's purposes. He wants us to pray, as Jesus did, "Not my will, but Thy will be done." Because His is the kingdom, the power, and the glory.

There is only one God, and we are not Him. As King and Creator, God calls the shots. It is only when we align ourselves underneath His comprehensive hand that we will access His full power and authority in all spheres of life: personal, familial, ecclesiastical, and governmental.

As we learn how to govern ourselves under God, we then transform the institutions of family, church, and society using a biblically based kingdom world view.

Under Him, we touch heaven and change earth.

To achieve our goal, we use a variety of strategies, approaches, and resources for reaching and equipping as many people as possible.

Broadcast Media

Millions of individuals experience *The Alternative with Dr. Tony Evans* through the daily radio broadcast playing on nearly **1,400 radio outlets** and in over **130 countries**. The broadcast can also be seen on several television networks and is available online at tonyevans.org. You can also listen to or view the daily broadcast by downloading the Tony Evans app for free in the App store. Over 30 million message downloads or streams occur each year.

Leadership Training

The Tony Evans Training Center (TETC) facilitates a comprehensive discipleship platform that embodies Dr. Tony Evans's ministry philosophy as expressed through the kingdom agenda. The training courses focus on leadership development and discipleship in the following five tracks:

- Bible and theology
- Personal growth
- Family and relationships
- Church health and leadership development
- Society and community impact strategies

The TETC program includes courses for both local and online students. Furthermore, TETC programming includes course work for non-student attendees. Pastors, Christian leaders, and Christian laity, both local and at a distance, can seek out the Kingdom Agenda Certificate for personal, spiritual, and professional development. For more information, visit tonyevanstraining.org.

Kingdom Agenda Pastors (KAP) provides a viable network for *like-minded pastors* who embrace the kingdom agenda philosophy. Pastors have the opportunity to go deeper with Dr. Tony Evans as they are given greater biblical knowledge, practical applications, and resources to impact individuals, families, churches, and communities. KAP welcomes *senior and associate pastors* of all churches. KAP also offers an annual summit held each year in Dallas with intensive seminars, workshops, and resources. For more information, visit kafellowship.org.

Pastors' Wives Ministry, founded by Dr. Lois Evans, provides *counsel*, *encouragement*, and *spiritual resources* for pastors' wives as they serve with their husbands in the ministry. A primary focus of the ministry is the KAP Summit that offers senior pastors' wives a safe place to *reflect*, *renew*, and *relax*, along with training in personal development, spiritual growth, and care for their emotional and physical well-being. For more information, visit loisevans.org.

Kingdom Community Impact

The outreach programs of the Urban Alternative seek to provide positive impact to individuals, churches, families, and communities through a variety of ministries. We see these efforts as necessary to our calling as a ministry and essential to the communities we serve. With training on how to initiate and maintain programs to adopt schools, or provide homeless services, or partner toward unity and justice with local police precincts, which creates a connection between the police and our community, we, as a ministry, live out God's kingdom agenda according to our Kingdom Strategy for Community Transformation.

The Kingdom Strategy for Community Transformation is a three-part plan that equips churches to have a positive impact on their communities for the kingdom of God. It also provides numerous practical suggestions for how this three-part plan can be implemented in your community, and it serves as a blueprint for unifying churches around the common goal of creating a better world for all of us. Visit tonyevans.org to access the three-part plan.

National Church Adopt-a-School Initiative (NCAASI) prepares churches across the country to impact communities by using *public schools as the primary vehicle for effecting positive social change* in urban youth and families. Leaders of churches, school districts, faith-based organizations, and other nonprofit organizations are equipped with the knowledge and tools to *forge partnerships* and build *strong social service delivery systems*. This training is based on the comprehensive church-based community impact strategy conducted by Oak Cliff Bible Fellowship. It addresses such areas as economic development, education, housing, health revitalization, family renewal, and racial reconciliation. We assist churches in tailoring the model to meet specific needs of their communities while simultaneously addressing the spiritual and moral frame of reference. Training events are held annually at Oak Cliff Bible Fellowship. For more information, visit churchadoptaschool.org.

Athlete's Impact (AI) exists as an outreach both into and through the sports arena. Coaches can be the most influential factor in young people's lives, even ahead of their parents. With the growing rise of fatherlessness in our culture, more young people are looking to their coaches for guidance, character development, practical needs, and hope. After coaches on the influencer scale fall athletes. Athletes (whether professional or amateur) influence younger athletes and kids within their spheres of impact. Knowing this, we have made it our aim to equip and train coaches and athletes on how to live out and utilize their God-given roles for the benefit of the kingdom. We aim to do this through our iCoach App as well as resources such as *The Playbook: A Life Strategy Guide for Athletes*. For more information, visit icoachapp.org.

Tony Evans Films ushers in positive life change through compelling video shorts, animation, and feature-length films. We seek to build kingdom disciples through the power of story. We use a variety of platforms for viewer consumption and have over 100 million digital views. We also merge video shorts and film with relevant Bible study materials to bring people to the saving knowledge of Jesus Christ and to strengthen the body of Christ worldwide. Tony Evans Films released the first feature-length film, *Kingdom Men Rising*, in April 2019 in over 800 theaters nationwide, in partnership with LifeWay Films. The second release, *Journey With Jesus*, is in partnership with RightNow Media.

Resource Development

We are fostering lifelong learning partnerships with the people we serve by providing a variety of published materials. Dr. Evans has published more than 125 unique titles based on over 50 years of preaching, including booklets, books, and Bible studies. He also holds the honor of writing and publishing the first full-Bible commentary and study Bible by an African American, released in 2019. This Bible sits in permanent display as a historic release in The Museum of the Bible in Washington, DC.

For more information, and a complimentary copy of Dr. Evans's devotional newsletter, call (800) 800-3222, write TUA at P.O. Box 4000, Dallas, TX 75208, or visit us online at www.tonyevans.org.

ACKNOWLEDGMENTS

I want to thank my friends at Baker Publishing Group for their interest and partnership in bringing my thoughts, study, and words to print on this valuable subject. I particularly want to thank Andy McGuire for leading the charge on this manuscript with Baker Publishing Group. It's been a pleasure working with Andy to see this through to print. I also want to publicly thank Sharon Hodge and Hannah Ahlfield. In addition, my appreciation goes out to Heather Hair for her skills and insights in writing and collaboration on not only this manuscript, but also on my book *Kingdom Man*.

NOTES

Day Two

1. *The Lord of the Rings: The Return of the King*, directed by Peter Jackson, screenplay by Fran Walsh, Philippa Boyens, and Peter Jackson (New Line Cinema, 2003), DVD.

Day Three

1. "The Legacy of a Man," Oak Cliff Bible Fellowship, accessed September 28, 2020, https://www.ocbfchurch.org/weekly-devotion/adam-where-you-at/the-legacy-of-a-man/.

Day Twenty-Nine

1. Jared Staver, "How Does Speed Affect Car Accident Damages," *Staver Legal Blog*, accessed September 21, 2020, https://www.chicagolawyer.com/speed-affect-car-accident-damages/.

Also from Tony Evans

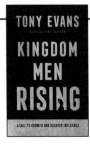

In his thought-provoking book, Dr. Tony Evans challenges you to foster personal discipleship and lead others, taking the next step to become the powerful man of God you were made to be. Evans brings his insights, stories, and wise counsel from God's Word to help you stop settling for a faith that goes through the motions and leave a legacy of faith.

Kingdom Men Rising

◈ BETHANYHOUSE

Stay up to date on your favorite books and authors with our free e-newsletters. Sign up today at bethanyhouse.com.

 facebook.com/BHPnonfiction

 @bethany_house

 @bethany_house_nonfiction